W0254624

Agricultural Prices in a Changing Economy

About the Author

Munish Alagh holds a doctoral degree from the School of Economics of Mumbai University and teaches at the AES Post Graduate Institute of Business Management of Ahmedabad University. His research on the agricultural economy of India, initially supervised by the late Manohar Rao and later Ajit Karnik, was a part of the School of Economics emphasis on researching the reform process at the macro and sectoral levels. An earlier paper on the Aggregate Supply Response Function in India was cited as a reference in discussions. Awarded the Vikram Sarabhai Trophy for the best student (1990-1993) of St. Xavier's College Ahmedabad, he won the CBP Award for the best research paper of Gujarat University (2004) and took additional credit in International Economics at Georgetown University, Washington, D.C.

Agricultural Prices in a Changing Economy

An Empirical Study of Indian Agriculture

MUNISH ALAGH

ACADEMIC FOUNDATION
NEW DELHI

www.academicfoundation.com

First published in 2011
by

ACADEMIC FOUNDATION
4772-73 / 23 Bharat Ram Road, (23 Ansari Road),
Darya Ganj, New Delhi - 110 002 (India).
Phones : 23245001 / 02 / 03 / 04.
Fax : +91-11-23245005.
E-mail : books@academicfoundation.com
www. academicfoundation.com

Cataloging in Publication Data--DK
Courtesy: D.K. Agencies (P) Ltd. <docinfo@dkagencies.com>

Alagh, Munish.
Agricultural prices in a changing economy : an empirical study of Indian agriculture / Munish Alagh.
p. cm.
Includes bibliographical references (p.).
Includes index.
ISBN 13: 9788171888108
ISBN 10: 8171888100

1. Agricultural prices--Government policy--India. 2. Produce trade--India. I. Title.

DDC 338.1854 22

Typeset by Italics India, New Delhi.
Printed and bound in India.

Contents

List of Tables and Figures

Tables

Figures

Foreword

This book entitled *Agricultural Prices in a Changing Economy,* by Munish Alagh critically examines how liberalisation of the economy initiated in 1991 has strengthened the role of markets and has made agricultural price policy the main instrument for not only determining area allocation among crops but also in increasing aggregate agricultural output. Alagh believes that market determined behaviour is expanding significantly and can now both explain larger parts of the agricultural economy and can be used for structural understanding, projections and policy analysis.

Alagh starts by reviewing the debate on the role of price policy among stalwarts like Dantwala, 1962, Raj Krishna, 1967, Chakarvarti, 1974, etc. But he tries to put the debate in its historical context.

For this, Alagh intertwines the discussion with a review of growth of agricultural economy in India. This is important since agricultural markets become important only when large surpluses become available. In a subsistence economy with limited surpluses, there is hardly any need for extensive agricultural markets.

It has taken a long time for agricultural surpluses to become available and agricultural markets to emerge in India. The creation of network of irrigation canals and tanks by the British during the mid 1920s was a major development. But Indian agriculture remained low yield and food-deficit agriculture for a long time even after Independence. It was the introduction of seed-fertiliser technology during the mid sixties that was instrumental in raising the yield and output levels of different both food and non-food crops and augmenting aggregate agricultural output. The increased arrival of marketed surpluses for food and non-food crops was instrumental in extending the role of the market. With the maturing of technology and its extension to different parts of India, the growth rates of yield and output of many food and non-food crops (particularly oilseeds) recorded unprecedented increases during 1980-1983 to 1990-1993 in many states and regions of India. This was made possible primarily by technology which played the dominant role, but the role of price policy was also supportive in promoting growth and new technology. It was for the first time during 1964 that the government assigned a positive role to prices. The minimum support prices were set at remunerative level. But more important, the producers were assured that they would get guaranteed minimum price for all the produce they bring to the market.

Numerous price response studies undertaken at that time indicated that the price response was much weaker and it was the non-price technological factors like irrigation, fertiliser which had a much higher explanatory power (Krishna, 1962; Narain, 1965; Askari and Cummings, 1976; Gulati and Kelly, 1999).

The initiation of economic reforms in 1991 was instrumental in extending the role of markets and prices. The new policy framework which consisted of changes in macroeconomic policy, adjustment of exchange rates, ending protection to industry, abolition of controls and licences was aimed at liberalising the economy and integrating it with the world economy. Ending of discrimination against tradable agriculture was envisaged as one the important consequence of these policy changes. Increased market incentives were expected to considerably benefit Indian farmers.

It was therefore widely believed that by removing some of the constraints that Indian farmers were facing in responding to the market incentives and by assigning a dominant role to markets and prices, economic liberalisation would be instrumental in freeing the agricultural markets and making them more responsive to price signals. Alagh agrees that the role of prices has certainly increased and he believes that in the post-reform era, price policy can be a potent policy variable for augmenting agricultural output.

Another important contribution of Alagh is to have carefully analysed some methodological deficiencies in the response functions used by numerous scholars. This he thinks may have been one of the reasons for elasticity pessimism. In this context, he has updated

Nerlovian models of acreage and price response, using causal chain specifications, which he finds has a much higher explanatory power. He believes that the use of similar techniques would be useful for the policy makers to include prices as one of the important variables for promoting agricultural growth. He is aware that in many regions of India infrastructural development may be necessary, but he no longer suffers from price elasticity pessimism and is more optimistic about the role of prices and terms of trade.

This is a very timely book which contains comprehensive examination of the issues related with the price responsiveness of agriculture and reviews the lively debate on the subject in a historical context. Researchers and policy makers will find the book very useful.

G.S. Bhalla
Professor Emeritus,
Jawaharlal Nehru University,
New Delhi

Preface

I spent half my growing up years and studies in Delhi and the rest in Western India, following a father who would get called to Delhi but not give up his academic nest in Ahmedabad. I shared Delhi's ideals but also remained intellectually ensconced in the markets of Western India. I chose to study serious economics in the School of Economics of Bombay University. Prof. Dilip Nachane taught and led a programme of research on the reform impact on the Indian economy. Together with Prof. Manohar Rao and colleagues like Prof. Abhay Pethe, Prof. Errol De Souza and Prof. Ajit Karnik, they ingrained in us that policy reform has consequences and cannot be ignored, but its impact needs deep study of instruments and targets. I took up the area of agriculture and after the usual drill of literature review wrote a piece on the aggregate supply function for Indian agriculture, which attempted new ground both in the elasticity debate, in empirical methods and in periodising the Indian economy. Those whom the gods love die young and my teacher M.J. Manohar Rao left us suddenly for his heavenly abode.

Prof. Ajit Karnik took over my early quest and put me through the paces which only a seasoned teacher can. In long e-mails and briefer visits to Mumbai I was criticised, provoked and my early ideas penciled through largely red and sometimes blue. This was done to my theory, my data, techniques and results. I grew up with economists who were giants in their own rights, the late D.T. Lakadawala, V.N. Dandekar were house guests. I had access to Profs. G.S. Bhalla and V.S. Vyas. Read and read more was the message and the traps of the past were made alive and placed in front of my feet. I knew the late Dr. D.S. Tyagi and Prof. S.L. Bapna, Prof. S.P. Kashyap, Prof. Rohit Desai and Prof. G.K. Chaddha gave me time. I always had access to Profs. Gerry Rodgers, R. Radhakrishna, S.R. Hashim, Atul Sarma and T.S. Papola. For a student of economics, truly formidable and humbling. But what a great education.

But most of all there is Yoginder K. Alagh, never willing to budge from his belief that markets work only if 'used' as a part of a strategic vision, but very catholic on data, theories and results. At heart a young teacher always critical on his terms, but reassuring when he is satisfied on mine. If he would raise his eyebrows I felt unfairly, I could always go to my mother Raksha and my friend, critic and elder sibling Tavishi. If still alone there was my dog Tipsy, alas no more.

I would also like to thank numerous other friends and relatives as well as my colleagues in AES Post Graduate Institute of Business Management now Ahmedabad University. You are of course all a part of me and so responsible for all the mistakes I make. Also, the glory of anything little I may have achieved.

Munish Alagh

1 Introduction

Introduction

There is a long tradition in Indian agricultural economics that works with the implicit or explicit assumption that Indian agriculture is largely peasant-based but on account of market imperfections, prices have a limited role to play. It is the argument of this work that this understanding needs modification. The economy has undergone growth and more important, its structure, policies and institutions are undergoing major changes. It would be exaggerated to say that the agricultural economy works under the paradigm of perfectly working market economies, since the economy itself is undergoing a transition path. Aspects of the agricultural economy still show low response to price stimuli. Also, institutions condition in important respects non-price behaviour. But market determined behaviour is expanding significantly and can now both explain larger parts of the agricultural economy and can be used for structural understanding, projections and policy analysis.

Elasticity pessimism was a dominant theme in the dominant earlier "meta" studies on the role of prices and markets in Indian agriculture. These studies either took a priori positions or were reflecting larger macro policy perspectives while analysing the agricultural sector. C.H. Hanumantha Rao (1975) for example with an encyclopedic understanding of Indian agriculture took the position that the technological base and distributive aspects of Indian agriculture determined economic outcomes. M.L. Dantwala analyses the relation between agriculture and the rest of the economy in development terms, actual and desired.

Prof. Dantwala reflects the dominant thinking then in giving prices an instrumental and behavioural role. He analyses the relation between agriculture and the rest of the economy in development, actual and desired. In a summary of a group discussion he says, "It was however agreed that the price policy could and should be utilised for the limited purpose of influencing specific situations or correcting a trend patently inconsistent with the objectives of planning." (Dantwala, 1962: 111)

At that phase of our reasoning, it was axiomatically assumed in academic discussion (See for example, Acharya and Agarwal, 1994) that in most countries, the necessity for the State to assume a leading role arose undoubtedly from the low level of agricultural production, wide prevalence of poverty and unemployment and perceived inadequacy of normal market forces to generate surpluses at a rapid rate to satisfy the basic aspirations of the people engendered by the end of foreign political domination.

In the late sixties and seventies, the dominant sense amongst influential Indian economists was that the aggregate agricultural supply function of the Indian economy was price inelastic. Chakravarty, 1974 treated the agricultural supply constraint as critical to the growth process. The argument was present in Dharam Narain (1965), Blyn (1966), Ashok Mitra (1977) and R. Thamarajakshi (1977). On the other hand, Dantwala represents an economist who was not unsympathetic to the role of the market and prices in resource allocation and efficiency in agriculture, and yet in the period remains a sceptic on price response.

Other authors more sympathetic to markets as resource allocators were also at the margin, raising doubts. For example, experts like A. Kahlon and D. Tyagi questioned if price response studies could give precise indications for price policies, given regional, crop and weather specificities (Kahlon and Tyagi, 1983: 24).

While the general tenor was critical on price responses, there were robust counterfactuals. Raj Krishna (1967) was one of the earlier economists who saw a more important role for prices in the agricultural economy in terms of resource allocation and efficiency. Beginning with Raj Krishna, studies like that by S.L. Bapna estimated that at least at the crop level, price response was positive (Bapna, 1980). Questions were also raised on the inelasticity pessimism debate. While earlier scholars like Rajbans Kaur (1984) gave a 'balanced' picture, by the late eighties there emerged a more elaborate literature questioning the elasticity pessimism of earlier scholars on aggregate supply response, in the work of V. Mishra and P. Hazell (1996) and others. Our approach, which is to examine the market responses of Indian agriculture in the reform period, builds on the tradition of these later studies and scholars.

The question we are examining is the response to prices at the aggregate level in the Indian agricultural economy, for that question is of relevance in the policy reform debate. There was an earlier debate on aggregate trends of production and productivity in Indian agriculture in the works of Prof. Dantwala and Prof. Hanumantha Rao but the good growth performance of the eighties is by now acknowledged (Vyas, 2003). However, the demand aspect as pushing growth is seen more recently. Also, the sub-sectoral aspects need to be placed in focus, since different elasticities of demand say of food grains and non-food grains, would underpin growth differently.

There are a number of analysis of the so called crisis of Indian agriculture since the nineties of the last century. The Ministry of Agriculture's *State of the Farmer* volumes bring this out including the volumes by Abhijit Sen, V.M. Rao, G.K. Chadha, G.S. Bhalla and B.B. Bhattacharya (MOA, 2004, Vols. XIV, X, II, XIX, XVIII) and the theme is again outlined in the Mid-Term Review of the Tenth Plan (Planning Commission, 2005). We can also outline this crisis by the work of Vyas, 2003a.

Our study initially examines the record of production and productivity change in Indian agriculture to set the backdrop of the main analysis of price responses. This is then followed by the development of policy tools more synchronous with the larger policy changes taking place in India.

Motivation of the Study

The motivation of the study is to find out the extent to which in terms of allocation of resources, output and productivity trends, the Indian agricultural economy shows the impact of price signals and response to market behaviour. The underlying assumption of the reform process is to postulate that the agricultural sector responds to market and price signals. Does empirical analysis verify the hypothesis that Indian agriculture responds at the aggregate level to price stimuli? Or does the agrarian economy reflect the transitional nature of the policy regime being followed, with some aspects responding to price signals and others determined by quantitative restrictions?

It is possible that allocation of resources to crops is price elastic only for the sectors where markets are allowed to function. This question arises since in food grains and external trade, there are still substantial government interventions, both of a quantitative and non-quantitative nature. It has long been accepted that at the crop level agriculture in India is price responsive. However, is it now true that there is a substantial sub-sector of the Indian agricultural economy which is price responsive? This kind of a hypothesis would be more substantive than the statement accepted for long that at the crop level, resource allocation was price sensitive. Do the underlying production, land allocation and productivity trends show that in the period of faster growth of the Indian economy and market reform, substantial agricultural sectors show the impact of income growth and of prices?

If the answer is positive to these questions, ignoring the marketisation of substantial sections of the economy will create both an understanding and a policy problem. We would then need to develop suitable systems which are explanatory tools in the transitional regime. These tools (models) could then be used for policy analysis, both of a forecasting nature as also of a normative welfare gains type.

Regarding the level and nature of growth in Indian agriculture, which is a backdrop to this work, it is instructive to look at previous works on agricultural growth and trends. There was in the sixties and seventies, an interesting debate between Dantwala and Hanumantha Rao. To introduce this, let us state this result from Dantwala, "The facts are that between 55-56 and 64-65, acreage under all commodities has increased by about 8 per cent and production by 34.8%." (Dantwala, 1967: 3). He states this in order to contradict the belief of some people that increase in production was due to the increase in acreage and since the scope for further expansion in acreage is limited, in future agricultural production may not increase at the same rate. However, from the mid-sixties this was precisely the case, Hanumantha Rao outlines, for example agricultural growth was technology and not economic incentive-driven. Thus:

"It was becoming clear by the mid sixties that there was no alternative to technological change in agriculture for achieving self-sufficiency in food grains." (Rao, 1975: 130). He underlines agricultural growth determined by the HYV technologies and investment in irrigation. And so: *"However owing to land constraint the growth of net sown area slowed down considerably"* (emphasis mine). This explains why despite the above steps the growth rate of agricultural output in the post green revolution period was broadly the same as in the pre green revolution period." (Ibid.: 131-132). The growth path is therefore, to an extent determined by natural resource constraints.

Dantwala quotes Hanumantha Rao as saying, "there are reasons to believe that even without the Green Revolution the growth rate would have been maintained at 2-2.5% per annum." (Dantwala, 1976: 43). This is due to the growth of population leading to an upward pressure on prices of agricultural commodities providing incentives to the farmer for expanding output and inducing the government to invest in irrigation, fertilisers, etc. However, Dantwala disagrees with this argument. According to him under static technology, high prices have little impact on aggregate production. He also says, "it is surprising that one so deeply concerned with poverty of the Indian masses should wish to rely on high food price path of growth of production instead of welcoming the cost reducing technology for achieving increased production!" (Ibid.: 43).

Hanumantha Rao, however, at this time continued to maintain this argument with the logic that, "some of these inputs including fertilisers which were known before the onset of the green revolution would have been used at a certain rate even in its absence." (*op.cit.*: 43). Dantwala, however, questions this argument too. His point being the well known one that application of higher doses of fertilisers to the traditional seeds led mainly to vegetative growth; also growth in cropped area was slowing down in the decade of the sixties as compared to the fifties. He comes to the conclusion that under the circumstances, adoption of high yielding varieties was the only solution to the food problem in the country.

Regarding the contemporary phase, according to V.S.Vyas, "The performance of the agricultural sector is all the more impressive once we realize that additions to the output have been realized by increases in yield per hectare rather than by an expansion of cultivated area, latter has remained more or less stable. It can be well appreciated that to obtain increases in production by intensive agriculture is much more difficult than raising additional output with the expansion of culturable area. The former requires not only a better access to non-land inputs, but also a much more careful use of these inputs." (Vyas, 2003: 43). We have already noted earlier that Vyas has, with others, being discussing the slowdown in Indian agriculture in the nineties.

Supply Pessimism

In the late sixties and seventies, the dominant sense amongst influential Indian economists was that the aggregate agricultural supply function of the Indian economy was price inelastic. S. Chakravarti treated the agricultural supply constraint as critical to the growth process. The argument was present in Dharam Narain (1965), Blynn (1966) and Mitra (1977), amongst others. Chakravarti states, using R. Thamarajakshi's work, "that income terms of trade have behaved against the industrial sector." (Chakravarti, 1974: 217). Noting that "the product wage rate has gone up relatively with corresponding decline in the profit margin of the non-agricultural sector" and that the savings rate would be adversely affected, Chakravarti identifies "the inelasticity of the marketed surplus of agriculture as the single most important barrier to growth." (Ibid.: 222). There was also the argument amongst influential Indian economists that while allocation to resources at the crop level can be price elastic, this need not be so at the level of the agricultural sector as a whole. (Chakravarty, 1974; Bapna, 1980).

There was the argument that the rate of growth of the urban industrial sector or modern non-agricultural sector depends on the size of the food surplus made available by the agricultural sector. "The price instrument can be used for augmenting the marketed supplies only if the market supply response is positive." (Kaur, 1984). On a theoretical analysis of the effect on marketed surplus of price change she argues. "A change in farm price influences marketed surplus through income and substitution effects. While the income effect of an increase in price is to decrease the marketed supply, the substitution effect tends to increase it so that the two effects of price change work in opposite directions and the total effect may not be clearly ascertainable in many cases." (Ibid., p.10).

The conclusion drawn from this is that an increase in farm prices may not necessarily bring an increased marketed surplus. Kaur has a fairly elaborate summary of the debates at that time. She quotes P.N. Mathur and H. Ezekiel to state that, "...the subsistence farmers who constitute a sizeable fraction of the farming community in many of the developing countries may have fixed cash requirements and under these circumstances the quantity sold may be smaller at higher prices." (Ibid., p.14). She summarises different studies arriving at different conclusions on the price sensitivity of marketed elasticity. Raj Krishna on the basis of his analysis ruled out the possibility of marketed surplus being negatively related to price. Thamarajakshi found that the relation between marketed surplus of all agricultural commodities and inter-sectoral terms of trade was not significant. Ms. Kaur concludes, "The evidence presented above, though somewhat conflicting suggests that market supply response is positive albeit weak." (Ibid.: 14). Rajbans Kaur was one of the first scholars in addition to Raj Krishna to moderate the earlier supply elasticity pessimism. For quite some time, however, alternate positions on the role of prices continued.

R. Thamarajakshi starts with a plea for positive price policy when she writes, "The contours of agricultural price policy for a densely populated, developing economy have to be delineated with the specific objective of maximising agricultural surpluses." However, she stresses the main objective of price policy in that era when she writes, "It may, however be noted that be it a negative price policy or a policy of incentive prices, the basic premise is that for an unhindered growth of the economy, large surpluses from the agricultural sector should be forthcoming." (Thamarajakshi, 1977: 376). She explains what is required from price policy. "In deploying a positive price policy, therefore, it is necessary not only to know the precise nature of the role of price mechanism in stimulating agricultural production but also to keep in view the overall and long run effects of increases in agricultural prices on saving, investment and production in the economy."

A cautionary note is given in the same paragraph, "The limits of a positive price policy need to be carefully noted lest this instrument be overstretched to inadvertently affect the very cause of growth for which it is employed." (Ibid.: 376).

Supply pessimism was one argument. But other scholars sympathetic to the benign role of the market were also sceptic regarding its efficacy. For example, Kahlon and Tyagi write:

"In any case for a price policy to be effective, it is necessary that the authorities must have a reliable estimate of the price elasticity of supply. Clearly, if the price elasticity is both positive and significant, the authorities may succeed in their goal. And by knowing the size of the elasticity coefficient the policy maker would have a precise idea as to what level of price support would be necessary" (Kahlon and Tyagi, 1983: 24). In this context Kahlon and Tyagi conclude from previous studies that:

"The supply elasticities especially the short run elasticities, though positive, were found to be of low magnitude for most of the major crops in India. These findings have the obvious policy implication that price, as an instrument for achieving increased production, may have only a limited role to play."(Ibid.: 25). In the eighties, however, the appreciation of the role of the market was widening. Kahlon and Tyagi, also see the role of markets in a larger setting and set up the broader themes for discussion:

"There remain, however, complex questions as to the factors influencing the levels of farmer response to prices. The relative roles of fluctuations in area and yield, the effect on production of technology and weather, and more importantly, the fluctuations in response among regions of widely differing physical, economic and social characteristics, have become issues to be settled by further theoretical and empirical studies. Also for developing an effective price policy, the precise role of prices in stimulating total agricultural production and individual crop production as well as the overall effects of prices on savings, investment and production is to be known" (Ibid.: 25).

It is important to annotate that Raj Krishna (1967) is seen as one of the earlier economists who saw a role for prices in the agricultural economy in terms of resource allocation and efficiency. Others who followed his tradition were Bapna, (1980) and later Hazell and Mishra, (1996). We will examine the more technical arguments later in their contributions to agricultural supply analysis. To avoid duplication, these important contributions are only annotated here.

Policy Structures

In the nineties, newer formulations on policy structures in developing economies questioned the role of the State, once the agricultural economy gained in depth and size (Tyagi, 1990). A study on managing of the food policy in India starts by saying that the most significant achievement of this policy has been a substantial increase in the economic and physical access to food. However, he also brings out the limitations. More than a decade ago, D.S. Tyagi foresaw the crisis of 2006, namely that India has been importing wheat at prices higher than those offered by way of the minimum support price and in fact, subsidising imported wheat to sell it in the domestic market. This then leads to substantial welfare loss to Indian farmers. Tyagi said, "It needs to be noted that when the prices of wheat were high in the domestic market, even if the government would have allowed free trade in wheat and other cereals no net import would have taken place. This would have happened even in years when the world market prices were lower than the domestic market prices as the landed cost of food grains would have been much higher than the prevailing prices in the domestic market. Similarly when the world market prices were higher than the domestic market prices despite there being an excess supply in the country no net export of wheat or rice would have taken place. Thus the operations of private trade through the use of the world market would not have been in a position to bring about the desired supply-demand balance" (Tyagi, 1990: 175).

The nineties also sees the introduction of open economy techniques in agricultural analysis. In the international literature, apart from general equilibrium models, there emerged studies of trade and its impact as also of trade instruments, including tariff and tax policies. Indian literature also takes cognisance of open economy implications, although it was largely critical of trade impacts. (Bhalla, 2004 and Bhattacharyya, 2004).

Objectives of the Study

The interrelated analytical and empirical issues which motivate the study are: first, the changing nature of Indian agriculture. This becomes a matter of delineation of output and productivity trends across time and between the earlier period until the mid-seventies or eighties and the period since; second, the changing composition of output.

The analysis of the past would delineate the diversification of output and whether the whole agricultural economy or parts of it are demand determined (by the faster growth of the economy in recent decades) or supply determined (technology and resource scarcities) or alternately by both in the sense of the working of markets. Here, prices would become important signallers for resource allocation and this would need to be worked out in an empirical context.

Finally, there is the question of newer policy sets which emerge from the analysis for the future. If prices are important, it should be possible to explain the past with them for the sectors in which they are important. To be non-trivial, this would have to be for a significant part of the agricultural economy. If these models work, it should also be possible to use models with prices to develop forecasts for the future. Finally, in the present stage of an open economy agriculture, economic analysis techniques, like the distribution of gains of trade between producers and consumers of trade policy reform, could be used to work out the welfare consequences of trade policies.

Data and Methodology

Data Sources

The aggregate supply function analysis and trend analysis in our work relies on official secondary data. Index numbers of area and production of all crops, food grains and non-food grains are as estimated by the Directorate of Economics and Statistics of the Department of Agriculture and Cooperation of the Ministry of Agriculture, Government of India (DESA). Net and gross irrigated area are also taken from the land use statistics released from the same source. Fertiliser consumption statistics are from the Fertiliser Association of India. All these estimates are presented in *Agricultural Statistics at a Glance*, published by DESA. Terms of trade data are taken from two sources. The first is the implied price deflators in *National Account Statistics*, published by the Central Statistical Organisation. Gross value of output in the agricultural sector at current prices divided by the gross value of output in the agricultural sector at constant prices gives the price deflator for the agricultural sector. A similar procedure gives estimates for the non-agricultural sector. The ratio of the two estimates of price deflators gives the terms of trade for the agricultural sector (TOTn). The other source of this variable is the Reports of the Commission on Agricultural Costs and Prices (CACP), which prepares and publishes the index of terms of trade between the agricultural and non-agricultural sectors (TOTc).

Methods

For the specification of economic relationships, the analytical methods we have used rely largely on economic theory as applied to agriculture and well-known results like relatively inelastic income and supply parameters and lagged responses to prices on account of agricultural supply calendars. These are used to specify the parameters of supply functions and market response behaviour. For example, lags are used to solve the econometric problems of causality by specifying causal chain systems in Herman Wold's book (Wold and Gureen, 1953; for more recent treatment see Behrman, 1968; Klien, 1962; Nerlove, 1969; Waugh, 1969).

To estimate the structure of change taking place in Indian agriculture in response to the pattern of economic growth, we use linear and semi-log trend analysis at the level of each crop. We cover a long period i.e., 1950 to 2004, and therefore, periodise it according to economic growth epochs. We use the Chow test to test if the periodisation postulated is in fact borne out by the data in terms of differential growth rates or different supply function parameters.

We develop two stylised policy experiments. The first is to use our work on the aggregate supply function to forecast supply of the non-food grains sub-sector of the Indian agricultural economy, to see if we can track the theoretical cycles of agricultural activity through empirical analysis. In the second example, we would use the structure of classical welfare analysis to model and obtain numerical gains and losses of Government intervention policies in an open economy in a partial equilibrium framework (Krugman and Obstfeld, 2000).

Plan of the Study and Chapter Scheme

In this chapter (Chapter I), apart from the introductory sections, there is the plan of the study in terms of the chapter scheme.

Chapter II—Indian Agriculture: Growth and Change

The approach of this chapter is descriptive. The trends in growth of area, production and yield are significantly different between the periods 1950/51 to 1975/76 and 1975/76 to 2003/04, the last year for which data are available at the requisite level of disaggregation. The crops covered under food grains are rice, wheat, coarse cereals, maize, pulses and *tur*. In the non-food grains sector, we cover oilseeds, groundnut, rapeseed and mustard, cotton, sugarcane and potato. Since the purpose is descriptive, we report both linear and logarithmic trend equations. The first describes an estimate of annual increase, the second gives compounded rate of growth.

The trends in growth of area, production and yield are significantly different between the periods 1950/51 to 1975/76 and 1975/76 to 2003/2004. The difference between the trends in the two periods is statistically tested for statistical significance using the Chow test (Gujarati, 1995: 263-265).

The significantly different supply features in the two periods suggest differential responses to economic stimuli in the period of slower growth of the economy and the faster growth period. Also they suggest that parts of the agrarian economy may respond in different ways to market signals, setting the stage for the analysis of aggregate supply.

Chapter III—Aggregate Agricultural Supply

We begin this chapter with a review of the technical literature. The emphasis is on models and empirical studies. We begin with the theoretical literature on aggregate supply analysis, particularly the question on lags in response to price stimuli in the agricultural sector emerging from the time period characteristics of crop production. Given the seasonal nature of agricultural production, supply comes with a lag, depending on the crop calendar. This characteristic of the agricultural economy is recognised at the textbook level and we summarise the main outlines of the received theory and recent developments.

We then review the Indian studies on the subject, laying out the arguments of the elasticity pessimists and optimists. We begin with the arguments presented by influential Indian economists that while allocation to resources at the crop level can be price elastic, this need not be so at the level of the agricultural sector as a whole. (Chakravarty, 1974; Bapna, 1980 and many others). The sometimes mildly different, at other times contrary arguments are also presented, by earlier work (Krishna, 1967; Kahlon and Tyagi, 1983) and more recent studies (Hazell and Mishra, 1996).

We give in some detail the theoretical analysis of aggregate supply, the Nerlovian specifications, the restatements by Koyck, Klein and others, the details of cobwebs, converging and explosive cobwebs and the simplifications of the causal chain systems. We also review recent applications of time lags and price responsiveness in empirical studies. While the global literature is rich, we also review Indian studies, the elasticity pessimists followed by the work of Raj Krishna and later Mishra and Hazel. Given this flavour of the debate and in the context of the wider developments in the Indian economy, which we have noted, we postulate that:

(a) price responsiveness does not determine supply expansion in the first traditional phase of Indian agriculture after Independence (the period 1950/1980) and that in this phase, the main drivers of growth were area and technology;

(b) in the period since then (1980 to 2003/04), price incentives determine the aggregate effort the farmer puts in the agricultural system, for those aspects of the economy in which price incentives are allowed to function and in this context the application by the farmer, from the choices available to him of technology, determines the supply outcomes; and

(c) for the food grains economy, which was dominated by government policy objectives, the economy has to be modelled in the framework of an autonomous policy regime.

After much experimentation, we find from the Nerlovian acreage response function equations estimated by us that, for the period 1981/1982 to 2003/04, the elasticity of acreage response to terms of trade of the CACP is reasonable at 1.02, instead of above 4 when the GDP deflator terms of trade were used. The lagged estimates for this period confirm the results.

The Supply Function

We postulate that the aggregate supply function for Indian agriculture would, in the light of the above analysis, consist of a price responsive non-food grains sector and a trend determined food grains sector with the farmer confident that government determined prices for grain would rise as in the past. The non-food grains supply function is recursively determined. This kind of relation is associated with H. Wold's 1953 work. (See a simplified description in Christ, 1966: 454-456.) The first decision the farmer makes in the light of market trends is to allocate land resources to non-food grains. After that from the available technologies, he choses his input basket. Acreage is determined by the Nerlovian relation and productivity by technical change.

Chapter IV—Policy Analysis

In this chapter, we first explain the traditional theory of economic policy in a simple fashion. We then review some of the policy literature, both at home and abroad. Finally, we give two applications of the tools developed in this work. We use the cobweb models developed in Ch. III to see if we can forecast aggregate non-food grain acreages and supply in

India and use a partial equilibrium analytical framework to work out the impact of market instruments like tariff policies and domestic price interventions in the cotton crop.

Policy Simulations

We attempt to illustrate our analysis of some empirical relationships in earlier chapters by stylised policy experiments. We use two experiments. The first is to use our work on the aggregate supply function to forecast supply of the non-food grains sub-sector of the Indian agricultural economy. The Commission on Agricultural Costs and Prices has already stated (CACP, 2000) that at the crop level, these supply models would work. In the second example, we use the structure of classical welfare analysis to model gains and losses of Government intervention policies in an open economy in a partial equilibrium framework.

Acreage Projections with Acreage Response

The log lin cobweb model actually anticipates the direction of change every year as shown in actual experience and to that extent is an interesting tool, in the sense it can forecast the nature of movement in acreage in the cycle i.e., whether there will be a contractionary or expansionary movement, and this is an analytical plus point. It is easy in theory to show that a cobweb depicts oscillations. It is difficult to numerically demonstrate them. Our model succeeds in tracking the cycles and this is an important result.

We estimate acreage from the lag equation and with the acreage and predicted yield figures from the trend line estimate the supply variable. Supply as estimated from the log lin and linear acreage response figures is estimated as a forecast variable. There was a cycle in the actual supply curve for non-food grains in the period 1997/98 to 2002/03. The supply curve using the log lin acreage response curve tracks this cycle in terms of downturns and recoveries but forecasts larger swings than the actual cycle.

The linear supply projection again catches the cyclical variations but the cycle is now largely damped and the terminal year is not below the originating year as in the actuals and as tracked by the log lin model.

Effects of Intervention Policies and the Economics of Open Policies

After setting the theoretical framework in partial equilibrium welfare setting, we give an example of cotton policies in India. We examine the impact of cotton support at home and imports with low tariffs in the year 1999/2000 and 2000/01. The impact of policies is worked out on producers and consumers with the conceptual quantities spelt out above. The import policies and domestic support policies lead to a loss to producers of around Rs. 1500 crore if the farm level price inclusive of trade and transport costs is taken into account. Imports depress the realisation to the farmer at his doorstep. The effect of imports is a small gain to consumers as the figures on impact on consumers brings out.

The argument is that in an era of large imports, particularly when the difference between domestic costs and prices and that in a foreign country from where imports are sourced is not large enough to be swamped by trade and transport margins, the impact of support prices can be counterbalanced by imports and the domestic producer can suffer losses from policies which simultaneously support domestic prices but permit imports. We model the effect of MSP on domestic prices both attempted and market prices which we have collected. But we also look at the empirically estimated farm gate price for this analysis of gains and losses.

Chapter V—Major Findings and Conclusions

Aspects of the agricultural economy still show low response to price stimuli. Also, institutions condition in important respects non-price behaviour. But market determined behaviour is expanding significantly and can now both explain larger parts of the agricultural economy and can be used for structural understanding, projections and policy analysis according to our study. These aspects are spelt out in summary but in an analytical form in this chapter, which also lists the limitations of the study and scope for further work.

2 Indian Agriculture

Growth and Change

Introduction

This work is an attempt at analysing market behaviour as the Indian economy goes through the process of reform and it concentrates on the agricultural sector. The agricultural sector is traditionally regarded as having low price responses. On the demand side, both income and price elasticities are low as compared to other commodities. On the supply side, while the sector is supposed to show short-run volatility, its long-run elasticities are again low. Also, as regards crop choices it is the agro-climatic regimes which determine possibilities.

In India on top of the basic factors, the sector was also subject to State policies in terms of price and quantity interventions in markets. Price policy attempted to determine output prices by the interventions of parastatals acting presumably to implement State policies. Also, prices of inputs as also quantities were determined by the State. This was true for seeds, fertilisers, pesticides and credit. International trade for the sector was also controlled, both in terms of imports and exports of agricultural output and inputs.

India is a big country so there are differences in resource endowments, what we call the agro-climatic environment, these differences are there in factors like soil, water availability both surface water and groundwater, climate which can mean temperature, rainfall both levels and variation. Also, population densities are different. In some areas like the Gangetic plain, there is very high density of population, in the hill areas or in the desert areas of Rajasthan, density of population is lower. All of these factors mean that cropping patterns will be different in different areas, also because these factors are of a long term or permanent nature there is a kind of basic stability in cropping patterns. They do change because of economic reasons or technological reasons but the change is slower. Another factor is, from the fifties onwards there have been great changes particularly from the sixties in technology, namely the seed fertiliser technology. But the technologies adopted are in different areas with different seeds and this is also true of different crops. This leads again to different cropping patterns and different rates of agricultural growth Cropping patterns depend on technological factors, economic factors and institutional factors.

The economic factors are to maximise expected returns and these returns will depend on prices of output and prices of inputs. Inspite of the non-price factors outlined, market reform would impact on factor use and output. The extent of control was not the same for all commodities. Also, there were changes in policies. In this introductory chapter we attempt to examine the underlying trends in output and productivity behaviour at the crop level.

We begin with an introduction to the overall picture. According to analysis reported, production is growing much faster since the eighties for the agricultural sector as a whole, as compared to earlier periods. In non-food grains the growth rate of production is even faster. For non-food grains the increase in growth rate of area was even faster in the period after the eighties as compared to the period between 1950 and 1980. This takes place somewhat dramatically in the overall context of a decline in growth of area of all crops in the second period. Area is not growing in case of all crops in the period after 1980 but production continues to grow, hence the growth source was yield.

This chapter begins with the macro story of faster growth of the agricultural sector and in particular the non-food grains sector since the eighties. Also, growth is sourced by yield in the eighties with area showing no growth. The agricultural sector is responding to faster economic growth by meeting the new demands. The second section on food grains covers wheat, rice and coarse cereals and pulses. Wheat was the crop of the first phase, just as rice is of the second phase. The coarse cereals and pulses are doing badly apart from a crop like maize where there is non-food demand. The third section covers non-food grain crops. In many crops, area growth is higher in the second phase.

The Big Story

At the very macro level the following estimates brings out the main story. The larger picture in terms of output and productivity growth and the shift away from food grains is shown in the following estimates:

Table 2.1

Production Trends of Agriculture and Area Trends of All Crops 1950/51 to 2003/04

(Annual Compound)

	1950-51 to 2003-04	*1950-51 to 1979-80*	*1980-81 to 2003-04*
Production Growth Rate of Agriculture	2.6	2.18	3.04
Area Growth Rate of All Crops	0.5	0.86	0.00

Growth rate of production goes up since the eighties for the agricultural sector as a whole. Output is now rising at 3.04 per cent compound annual as compared to 2.18 per cent compound annual earlier. There is no contribution of area in the second phase, yield being the only source of growth. As we examine below, from the early fifties to the mid-seventies, food grains growth is 2.69 per cent annual and goes down to 2.25 per cent annual in the second phase. Area growth which was 0.86 per cent annual in the first phase goes down to a negative figure of minus 2.15 per cent annual in the second phase. Area allocation to non-food grains is the same as for food grains in the first phase but in the second phase area under food grains is falling and that under non-food grains is rising.

In terms of trends (Deshpande *et al.*, 2004), in their authoritative review of agricultural production in the last half century describe the trends that emerged as follows:

"The growth patterns in the crop economy have been analysed by many distinguished academicians in the last three decades (Bhalla and Alagh, 1979; Bhardwaj, 1982; Sawant and Achutan, 1995; Bhalla and Singh, 2002). We intend to pick up only a few major trends from these sources in this section. The growth in the crop economy came mainly through food grains in the two decades ending at 1990-91. The production in food grains grew at 2.63 per cent per annum during 1960-

70 and at 3.31 per cent per annum during 1980-90. The decade of eighties seemed to be a landmark decade in boosting up food grain production and the growth in food grains came mainly through increase in productivity. Haryana, Punjab, Uttar Pradesh and Rajasthan showed significantly higher growth compared to the rest of the country.

It is well known that wheat and paddy could consolidate the gains of technological change at the first instance. This was followed by maize, *jowar*, *ragi* and *bajra*. Thus, initially, the technological change helped the wheat and paddy growing farmers. According to the Agricultural Census 1970-71, the farmers growing paddy constituted about 22.86 per cent as against 11.56 per cent holdings having wheat. About 71 per cent of the total holdings were cereal dependent, whereas other 29 per cent grew non-food grains. Thus, the technological change of late sixties was mainly addressed to these 71 per cent farms. During the subsequent censuses the shares of area allocated to various crops underwent changes. If one matches these changes with the technological change a few interesting findings are confronted. First, the growth in productivity does not induce area allocation as a rule, but there are instances where area under crops has increased keeping in view the productivity growth. Second, the emphasis on food grains has been going down over the decades and more sharply during the later part of the five decades. Consequently, the area allocation towards commercial crops is increasing. Third, fruits and vegetables have been gaining significantly over the three decades at the cost of coarse cereals and pulses. Lastly, it is clear that on the eve of liberalisation 83.4 per cent of the small and marginal farmers and 68.19 per cent of the large farmers were growing food grains. Consequently, only about 17 per cent of the marginal and small farmers and 22 per cent of the large farmers involve themselves with commercial crops" (Deshpande *et al.*, 2004: 55-56).

Output trends were a source of concern since long. Thus, M.L. Dantwala wrote many decades ago, "Agricultural performance in the pre-independence period was far from satisfactory this was clearly stated in George Blyn's study of agriculture between 1891 and 1947. In fact according to this study—between 1911 and 1941, per capita availability of food grains—taking into account international trade flows-declined by as much as 26 per cent" (Dantwala, 1976: 31).

As far as agricultural growth was concerned it took off from this period onwards and Dantwala said, "Equally germane to the assessment of agriculture's production performance is the fact that in these two decades (1951-1971), India's population has increased by 187 million, and by 1976 another 60 million have been added. It is worth noting that in spite of this tremendous increase, this backward agriculture has been able to provide a per capita availability with marginal imports—at about 450 grams per day" (Ibid.: 32). But Dantwala warned even then "According to a 'medium' projection, by the end of the century, India's population will be about 1,000 million. Making a few balanced assumptions regarding the growth of population, growth rate of national income and its (more equitable) distribution, V.M. Rao has estimated that by the year 2001, India's requirements of food grains (assuming low population growth) would be 2.5 times its consumption in 1964-65; requirements of other foods would be as high as 4.35 times" (Ibid.: 32).

More recently, M.S. Swaminathan has this laudatory assessment, "Because of our policy of ensuring minimum support price to basic food crops through the Food Corporation of India, as well as State food corporations, the production of wheat and rice increased steadily and in 2001-02, the Government of India had food stocks exceeding 60 million tons. This enabled the government to initiate several food for work programs to insulate the poor from hunger." On the flip side, he says, "Inspite of our agricultural progress and food safety net programs, we now have as many children, women and men suffering from poverty induced hunger as the entire population in 1947" (Swaminathan, 2006, Foreword, pp.xi, xii).

According to Vyas, "The performance of the agricultural sector is all the more impressive once we realise that additions to the output have been realised by increases in yield per hectare rather than by an expansion of cultivated area, latter has remained more or less stable. It can be well appreciated that to obtain increases in production by intensive agriculture is much more difficult than raising additional output with the expansion of culturable area. The former requires not only a better access to non-land inputs, but also a much more careful use of these inputs" (Vyas, 2003a: 43).

R.S. Deshpande has recently reviewed trends in crop production since the sixties and introduces his book with a realisation that India's agricultural sector is presently at crossroads with the advent of the new forces in policy and trade sector:

"The sensitivity of the overall growth of the economy to the fluctuations in the agricultural sector is indisputable despite the less than 30 per cent share of agriculture in GDP" (Deshpande *et al.*, 2004: 37). He brings into focus, the many expectations from the sector by listing them out the onus of maintaining a consistent rate of growth, provision of food security to the millions below poverty line, contributing to the overall development scenario and participating in the global trade are prominent among them. The growth performance of agricultural sector is dictated mainly by four constituents according to him, *viz.*, farmer, land, crops and crop enterprises. "Any analysis of the sector, therefore, should account for the growth stimuli offered by these constituents as well as their responses to the policy tools. The situation gets further complex when we consider another perspective i.e. the non-homogeneity of each of them and their inter-relationships in addition to the outward linkages with the policy interventions. When we do this Crop enterprises and the farmer become the hub point of such understanding" (Ibid.: 37). To sum up in his words, "Analysing the performance of agricultural sector thus essentially involves tracking the changes along with these components and to understand the transition in agrarian economy from a farmer's perspective. After five decades of independence and planning, it is quintessential now to look back and learn from the past about our achievements and failures." (Ibid.: 37).

Crop-Wise Details

Food Grains

Table 2.2a shows the structure of food grains production since the mid-sixties.

The dominant impression from Table 2.2a is that of a remarkable underlying stability in area and a rapid increase in yield. The latter is particularly so from the mid-sixties. Since the mid-seventies yield almost doubles. Area is constant in the period from 1966/1968 to 2003/

2004, declining in the *Kharif* and rising in the *Rabi*. These results are influenced by the drought of 2002/03, when area went down to 113.86 million hectares. In the triennium 2000/01, area was higher at 124.12 million hectares. This is commented upon subsequently. *Rabi* shares of production has been rising.

Table 2.2a

Food Grains Area Production and Yield since the Mid-Sixties

(Area in million hectares; Production in million tonnes; Yield in kgs/hec)

	3-YR AVG 1966-1968	3-YR AVG 1974-1976	3-YR AVG 2002-2004
Kharif			
Area	79.85	81.45	71.53
Production	54.83	66.50	102.48
Yield	685.50	815.00	1428.00
Rabi			
Area	38.51	43.19	47.58
Production	29.82	43.94	95.14
Yield	771.00	1,016.00	1998
Total			
Area	118.36	124.63	119.11
Production	84.65	110.43	197.61
Yield	713.50	884.00	1656.33

Output of food grains increased annually by 2.08 million tonnes between 1950/51-1975/76 but went up by three quarters to an annual growth figure of 3.55 million tonnes in the period 1975/76-2002/03. (Table 2.2b). However, the compound growth rate was between 2.25 per cent to 2.69 per cent annual in the two periods. In the first period the growth of area was around 0.86 per cent annual and the yield growth rate was 1.82 per cent annual. In the second period, area stoped growing and the annual growth rate was negative and the entire expansion of output is from yield growth which went up from 1.81 per cent annual in the period 1950/1975 to 2.48 per cent annual in the period 1975/2003. Area increased in the first period significantly by 1.01 million hectares per year and declined by 0.27 million hectares per year in the second period. Yield increase of food grains per year was almost three times more in 1975-1976 to 2002/03 at 31.31 kg/ha per year as compared to 12.46 kg/ha per year in 1950-51 to 1974-75. Thus, yield expansion which was around 13 kgs per hectare in the first period rose to around 32 kgs per hectare in the second period.

In the second period we see the interesting phenomenon of a much higher quantum of grains being produced with some land being actually released for other non-food grain crops. This takes place on account of a rapid increase in yield. Indian agriculture comes of age with diversification of the cropping base in relation presumably to demand arising from faster economic growth within the context of limited land reserves.

Table 2.2b

Area, Production and Yield Trends of Food Grains 1950/51 to 2003/04

Food grains		*Production*			*Area*			*Yield*		
		1950-51 to 2003-04	*1950-51 to 1974-75*	*1975-76 to 2003-04*	*1950-51 to 2003-04*	*1950-51 to 1974-75*	*1975-76 to 2003-04*	*1950-51 to 2003-04*	*1950-51 to 1974-75*	*1975-76 to 2003-04*
Linear	b	3.05	2.08	3.55	0.33	0.96	-0.27	23.17	12.46	31.31
	t	33.1	11.66	14.93	6.60	10.22	-4.41	28.75	10.30	21.60
Compound	b	2.6	2.69	2.25	0.29	0.86	-2.15	2.30	1.81	2.48
	t	36.97	11.16	14.35	6.58	9.66	-14.37	41.08	10.25	20.07

Note: Units as in Table 2.2a; b: annual growth rate; t: t-statistic.

Table 2.2c depicts tests of significance of differences of growth rate in the two periods using the Chow test. (Gujarati, 1995: 263-265). This test is as follows:

If the trend estimate for period I is:

$Y_{t=} a_1+a_2t+u_{1t}$ $t=1,2,....n_1$

that for period II is

$Y_{t=}b_1+b_2t+u_{2t}$ $t=1,2,....n_2$

and for the combined period n_1 and n_2 the estimate is

$Y_{t=}c_1+c_2t+u_t$

The residual sum of squares of the third regression is say S_1 with $d_f=(n_1+n_2\text{-}k)$

Similarly S_2 is for the first estimate and S_3 for the second. Then if

$S_4=S_2+S_3$ with $df=n_1+n_2-2k$

Estimate

$S_5=S_1-S_4$

The Chow test is performed with

$$F=\frac{S_5/k}{S_4/(n_1+n_2-2k)}$$

Table 2.2c shows that the growth rates are significantly different between the two periods, apart from the exponential growth rate in output, which is not significantly different.

Table 2.2c

Tests of Significance of Growth Rate Differences in the Periods 1950-51 to 1974-75 and 1975-76 to 2003-04

	1950-51 to 2003-04	*1950-51 to 1974-75*	*1975-76 to 2003-04*
	Production		
Linear Trend Coefficient	3.048	2.079	3.549
t-statistic	33.1	11.66	14.93
Chow Test	$S_1=5784.68$; $S_2=951.07$; $S_3=3096.59$; $S_4=4047.66$; $S_5=1737.02$; $F=\frac{(1737.02/2)}{(4047.66/50)}=10.729$		
	The value exceeds critical value of $F_{2,50}$ i.e., 3.2, rejecting the hypothesis of no difference in the growth for the two periods.		
Exponential Trend Coefficient	1.0260	1.0269	1.0225
t-statistic	36.97	11.16	14.35
Chow Test	$S_1=0.32855$; $S_2=0.16898$; $S_3=0.13230$; $S_4=0.30128$; $S_5=0.02727$; $F=\frac{(0.02727/2)}{(0.30128/50)}=2.26$		
	The value is less than critical value of $F_{2,50}$ i.e., 3.2, not rejecting the hypothesis of no difference in the growth for the two periods.		
	Area		
Linear Trend Coefficient	0.331	1.009	-2.66
t-statistic	6.60	1141.2	-4.41

contd...

...*contd*...

	1950-51 to 2003-04	*1950-51 to 1974-75*	*1975-76 to 2003-04*
Chow Test	$S_1 = 1713.36;\ S_2 = 0.023;\ S_3 = 199.319;\ S_4 = 199.34;$ $S_5 = 1514.02;\ F = \frac{(1514.02/2)}{(199.34/50)} = 189.88$ The value exceeds critical value of $F_{2,50}$ i.e., 3.2, rejecting the hypothesis of no difference in the growth for the two periods.		
Exponential Trend Coefficient	1.0029	1.0086	0.9978
t-statistic	6.58	9.66	-14.37
	Yield		
Linear Trend Coefficient	23.170	12.462	31.309
t-statistic	28.75	10.30	21.60
Chow Test	$S_1 = 443149.18;\ S_2 = 43786.15;\ S_3 = 115148.34;$ $S_4 = 158934.49;$ $S_5 = 284214.69;\ F = \frac{(284214.69/2)}{(158934.49/50)} = 44.71$ The value exceeds critical value of $F_{2,50}$ i.e., 3.2, rejecting the hypothesis of no difference in the growth for the two periods.		
Exponential Trend Coefficient	1.0230	1.0181	1.0248
t-statistic	41.08	10.25	20.07
Chow Test	$S_1 = 0.20990;\ S_2 = 0.09190;\ S_3 = 0.08137;$ $S_4 = 0.17327;$ $S_5 = 0.03653;\ F = \frac{(0.03653/2)}{(0.08137/50)} = 5.27$ The value exceeds critical value of $F_{2,50}$ i.e., 3.2, rejecting the hypothesis of no difference in the growth for the two periods.		

Rice

In rice, area growth continues in the second period also as Table 2.3a shows. Output at 88.78 million tonnes in the triennium ending 2000, almost doubled, by the end nineties but then fell and was 91 per cent higher in the second phase largely from productivity growth.

Output of rice increased annually by .871 million tonnes between 1950/51-1974/75, but went up by double to an annual growth figure of 1.66 million tonnes in the period 1975/76-2003/04 (Table 2.3b). However, the compound growth rate was between 2.57 per cent to 2.79

per cent annual in the two periods. In the first period, the growth of area was around 1.06 per cent annual and the yield growth rate was 1.71 per cent annual. In the second period area stops growing and the expansion of output is from yield growth which went up from 1.71 per cent annual in the period 1950/1975 to 2.13 per cent annual in the period 1975/2003. Area increased in the first period significantly by .36 million hectares per year and by 0.18 million hectares per year in the second period. Yield increase of rice per year was almost two times more in 1975-76 to 2003/04 at 32.92 kg/ha per year as compared to 15.59 kg/ha per year in 1950-51 to 1975-76. Thus, yield expansion which was around 16 kgs per hectare in the first period rose to around 32 kgs per hectare in the second period.

Table 2.3a

Area, Production and Yield of Rice From 1950-51 and 2001-2003

(Area in million hectares; Production in million tonnes; Yield in kgs/hec)

	3 YR AVG 1950-1952	*3 YR AVG 1974-1976*	*3 YR AVG 2001-2003*
Area	30.32	38.69	42.86
Production	20.94	44.16	84.48
Yield	691	1140.00	1966.67

Table 2.3b

Area, Production and Yield Trends of Rice 1950/51 to 2003/04

Rice		*Production*			*Area*			*Yield*		
		1950-51 to 2003-04	*1950-51 to 1974-75*	*1975-76 to 2003-04*	*1950-51 to 2003-04*	*1950-51 to 1974-75*	*1975-76 to 2003-04*	*1950-51 to 2003-04*	*1950-51 to 1974-75*	*1975-76 to 2003-04*
Linear	b	1.31	0.87	1.66	0.26	0.36	0.18	25.12	15.59	32.92
	t	27.41	10.98	13.25	25.80	18.57	7.31	25.42	7.65	14.09
Compound	b	2.68	2.79	2.57	0.71	1.06	0.44	1.96	1.71	2.13
	t	32.80	10.44	12.34	23.45	17.59	7.28	28.48	7.38	12.87

Note: Units as in Table 2.3a; b: annual growth rate; t: t-statistic.

Table 2.3c shows that the linear trends of production area and yield are different between the two periods but the exponential trends are not.

Table 2.3c

Tests of Significance of Growth Rate Differences in the Periods 1950-51 to 1974-75 and 1975-76 to 2003-04

	1950-51 to 2003-04	*1950-51 to 1974-75*	*1975-76 to 2003-04*
	Production		
Linear Trend Coefficient	1.31	0.87	1.66
t-statistic	27.41	10.98	13.25
Chow Test	$S_1 = 1558.165$; $S_2 = 188.047$; $S_3 = 863.820$; $S_4 = 1051.867$; $S_5 = 506.298$; $F = \frac{(506.298/2)}{(1051.867/50)} = 12.03$ The value exceeds critical value of $F_{2,50}$ i.e., 3.2, rejecting the hypothesis of no difference in the growth for the two periods.		
Exponential Trend Coefficient	1.027	1.028	1.026
t-statistic	32.80	10.44	12.34
Chow Test	$S_1 = 0.44450$; $S_2 = 0.20806$; $S_3 = 0.23263$; $S_4 = 0.44069$; $S_5 = 0.00381$; $F = \frac{(0.00381/2)}{(0.44069/50)} = 0.216$ The value is less than critical value of $F_{2,50}$ i.e., 3.2, not rejecting the hypothesis of no difference in the growth for the two periods.		
	Area		
Linear Trend Coefficient	0.26	0.36	0.18
t-statistic	25.80	18.57	7.31
Chow Test	$S_1 = 71.230$; $S_2 = 11.283$; $S_3 = 34.118$; $S_4 = 45.401$; $S_5 = 25.829$; $F = \frac{(25.829/2)}{(45.401/50)} = 14.22$ The value exceeds critical value of $F_{2,50}$ i.e., 3.2, rejecting the hypothesis of no difference in the growth for the two periods.		
Exponential Trend Coefficient	1.01	1.01	1.00
t-statistic	23.45	17.59	7.28
	Yield		
Linear Trend Coefficient	25.12	15.59	32.92
t-statistic	25.42	7.65	14.09

contd...

...contd...

	1950-51 to 2003-04	1950-51 to 1974-75	1975-76 to 2003-04
Chow Test	$S_1 = 666259.77$; $S_2 = 124282.51$; $S_3 = 299156.74$; $S_4 = 423439.25$; $S_5 = 242820.52$; $F = \frac{(24220.52/2)}{(423439.25/50)} = 14.34$ The value exceeds critical value of $F_{2,50}$ i.e., 3.2, rejecting the hypothesis of no difference in the growth for the two periods.		
Exponential Trend Coefficient	1.1	1.01	1.02
t-statistic	28.48	7.38	12.87
Chow Test	$S_1 = 0.31760$; $S_2 = 0.15794$; $S_3 = 0.14644$; $S_4 = 0.30438$; $S_5 = 0.01322$; $F = \frac{(0.01322/2)}{(0.30438/50)} = 1.08$ The value is less than critical value of $F_{2,50}$ i.e., 3.2, thus not rejecting the hypothesis of no difference in the growth for the two periods.		

Wheat

Wheat was the crop in which the Green Revolution began. Area doubles in the first phase (Table 2.4a) while Area growth in the second phase is lower. It was as we saw higher in rice in that phase. Rice was the crop of the second phase. Output of wheat goes up by more than four times in the first phase and then the growth is less but is still high. Productivity roughly doubles in each phase.

Table 2.4a

Area, Production and Yield of Wheat 1950/51 to 2001/2003

(Area in million hectares; Production in million tonnes; Yield in kgs/hec)

	3 YR AVG 1950-1952	3 YR AVG 1974-1976	3 YR AVG 2001-2003
Area	9.61	19.01	26.04
Production	6.32	27.32	70.21
Yield	658	1378	2695

Table 2.4b shows the same picture in growth rates. The annual growth in area in the first phase is a little over thrice the second phase, going down from 2.73 per cent compound annual to 0.85 per cent annual. The annual production increase in the second period is 1.7 million tonnes as compared to the figure of 0.79 million tonnes in the

first period. Growth of output in the first phase was 5.9 per cent annual and falls to 3.49 per cent annual in the second phase. Area growth in the first phase was over 2.73 per cent annual and falls sharply in the second phase. The annual yield increase in the second phase is impressive at 52.8 kgs/hec but the yield growth rate also goes down, from 3.06 per cent annual to 2.61 per cent annual. Wheat is definitely the crop of the late sixties and seventies, just as rice is of the second period i.e.,1975-76/2003-04.

Table 2.4b

Area, Production and Yield Trends of Wheat 1950/51 to 2003/04

Wheat		*Production*			*Area*			*Yield*		
		1950-51 to 2003-04	*1950-51 to 1974-75*	*1975-76 to 2003-04*	*1950-51 to 2003-04*	*1950-51 to 1974-75*	*1975-76 to 2003-04*	*1950-51 to 2003-04*	*1950-51 to 1974-75*	*1975-76 to 2003-04*
Linear	b	1.42	0.79	1.70	0.35	0.38	0.20	44.76	28.89	52.80
	t	34.73	10.15	23.70	29.03	11.81	11.44	36.94	9.45	24.14
Compound	b	5.14	5.90	3.49	1.99	2.73	0.85	3.09	3.06	2.61
	t	36.06	13.51	20.71	22.94	12.75	11.57	39.40	10.17	20.08

Note: Units as in Table 2.4a; b: annual growth rate; t: t-statistic.

Table 2.4c shows that in wheat the growth rate differences in area, production and yield are statistically significantly different between the two periods.

Table 2.4c

Tests of Significance of Growth Rate Differences in the Periods 1950-51 to 1974-75 and 1975-76 to 2003-04

	1950-51 to 2003-04	*1950-51 to 1974-75*	*1975-76 to 2003-04*
	Production		
Linear Trend Coefficient	1.419	0.791	1.698
t-statistic	34.73	10.15	23.70
Chow Test	$S_1 = 1138.947$; $S_2 = 182.031$; $S_3 = 281.154$; $S_4 = 463.185$; $S_5 = 675.762$; $F = \frac{(675.762/2)}{(463.185/50)} = 36.47$ The value exceeds critical value of $F_{2,50}$ i.e., 3.2, rejecting the hypothesis of no difference in the growth for the two periods.		

contd...

...contd...

	1950-51 to 2003-04	*1950-51 to 1974-75*	*1975-76 to 2003-04*
Exponential Trend Coefficient	5.135	5.900	3.488
t-statistic	36.06	13.51	20.71
Chow Test	$S_1 = 1.31519$; $S_2 = 0.53817$; $S_3 = 0.15022$; $S_4 = 0.68839$; $S_5 = 0.62780$; $F = \frac{(0.62780/2)}{(0.68839/50)} = 22.76$ The value is exceeds critical value of $F_{2,50}$ i.e., 3.2, rejecting the hypothesis of no difference in the growth for the two periods.		
	Area		
Linear Trend Coefficient	0.351	0.375	0.204
t-statistic	29.03	11.81	11.44
Chow Test	$S_1 = 99.738$; $S_2 = 30.171$; $S_3 = 17.359$; $S_4 = 47.530$; $S_5 = 52.208$; $F = \frac{(52.208/2)}{(47.530/50)} = 27.46$ The value exceeds critical value of $F_{2,50}$ i.e., 3.2, rejecting the hypothesis of no difference in the growth for the two periods.		
Exponential Trend Coefficient	1.990	2.726	0.853
t-statistic	22.94	12.75	11.57
	Yield		
Linear Trend Coefficient	44.76	28.893	52.804
t-statistic	36.94	9.45	24.14
Chow Test	$S_1 = 1001830$; $S_2 = 278962.6$; $S_3 = 262299.8$; $S_4 = 541262.4$; $S_5 = 460567.6$; $F = \frac{(460567.6/2)}{(541262.4/50)} = 21.27$ The value exceeds critical value of $F_{2,50}$ i.e., 3.2, rejecting the hypothesis of no difference in the growth for the two periods.		
Exponential Trend Coefficient	3.087	3.064	2.613
t-statistic	39.40	10.17	20.08
Chow Test	$S_1 = 0.40625$; $S_2 = 0.26315$; $S_3 = 0.09042$; $S_4 = 0.35357$; $S_5 = 0.05268$; $F = \frac{(0.05268/2)}{(0.35357/50)} = 3.72$ The value exceeds critical value of $F_{2,50}$ i.e., 3.2, thus rejecting the hypothesis of no difference in the growth for the two periods.		

Coarse Cereals

There has been through the half century a movement away from coarse cereals. This is largely taste and income determined since these are Giffen goods. (Sen, 2005). However, it is also true that coarse cereals were a dry land crop and productivity in the dry land areas did not keep pace, both on account of infrastructural bottlenecks and technological neglect. (Rao, 2004). Area under coarse cereals goes up in the first phase from 38.28 million hectares in the triennium 1950/1952 to 43.48 million hectares in the triennium 1974/1976. However, by the first triennium in this century (2001/2003), area under coarse cereals at 29.11 million hectares is less than in the early fifties. Output, however, doubles in the half century, going up from 15.74 million tonnes in the early fifties to 28.27 million tonnes in the mid-seventies and is at 32.52 million tonnes by the end of the period. Yield goes up from 4.11 qtls/hec to 6.5 qtls/hec and stood at 1112 kgs/hec at the end of the period.

Table 2.5a

Area, Production and Yield of Coarse Cereals 1950/51 to 2001/2003

(Area in million hectares; Production in million tonnes; Yield in kgs/hec)

	3 YR AVG 1950-1952	3 YR AVG 1974-1976	3 YR AVG 2001-2003
Area	38.28	43.48	29.11
Production	15.74	28.27	32.52
Yield	411	650	1112

Production growth declines sharply in the second period, both in the linear estimates and in the compound growth formulation. Area growth at a low level in the first phase (0.4 per cent annual) is negative in the second period at minus 1.65 per cent annual compound. This dominates and so area growth in the entire period is negative. (This is a mirage since the growth rates in the two periods are significantly different.) Yield expansion in terms of growth rates is much higher in the second period and compensates for the shrinking area.

Table 2.5c shows that the growth, area and productivity record is significantly different between the two periods apart from the compound growth of productivity which is not significantly different.

Table 2.5b

Area, Production and Yield Trends of Coarse Cereals 1950/51 to 2003/04

Cereals		Production			Area			Yield		
		1950-51 to 2003-04	1950-51 to 1974-75	1975-76 to 2003-04	1950-51 to 2003-04	1950-51 to 1974-75	1975-76 to 2003-04	1950-51 to 2003-04	1950-51 to 1974-75	1975-76 to 2003-04
Linear	b	0.25	0.39	0.11	-0.29	0.17	-0.59	12.70	6.96	17.46
	t	10.14	6.34	1.65	-9.91	3.23	-20.39	20.01	7.22	10.29
Compound	b	0.99	1.77	0.34	-0.78	0.40	-1.65	1.79	1.35	2.02
	t	10.04	6.26	1.57	-9.92	3.23	-18.99	25.39	7.30	10.52

Note: Units as in Table 2.5a; b: annual growth rate; t: t-statistic.

Table 2.5c

Tests of Significance of Growth Rate Differences in the Periods 1950-51 to 1974-75 and 1975-76 to 2003-04

	1950-51 to 2003-04	1950-51 to 1974-75	1975-76 to 2003-04
	Production		
Linear Trend Coefficient	0.254	0.391	0.111
t-statistic	10.14	6.34	1.65
Chow Test	$S_1 = 426.66;\ S_2 = 113.790;\ S_3 = 245.667;\ S_4 = 359.457;$ $S_5 = 67.203;\ F = \frac{(67.203/2)}{(359.457/50)} = 4.67$ The value exceeds critical value of $F_{2,50}$ i.e., 3.2, rejecting the hypothesis of no difference in the growth for the two periods.		
Exponential Trend Coefficient	0.990	1.768	0.341
t-statistic	10.04	6.26	1.57
Chow Test	$S_1 = 0.65570;\ S_2 = 0.23450;\ S_3 = 0.25927;\ S_4 = 0.49377;$ $S_5 = 0.16193;\ F = \frac{(0.16193/2)}{(0.49377/50)} = 8.20$ The value exceeds critical value of $F_{2,50}$ i.e., 3.2, rejecting the hypothesis of no difference in the growth for the two periods.		
	Area		
Linear Trend Coefficient	-0.290	0.169	-0.590
t-statistic	-9.91	3.23	-20.39

contd...

...contd...

	1950-51 to 2003-04	*1950-51 to 1974-75*	*1975-76 to 2003-04*
Chow Test	$S_1 = 584.424$; $S_2 = 81.837$; $S_3 = 45.912$; $S_4 = 127.749$; $S_5 = 456.675$; $F = \frac{(456.675/2)}{(127.749/50)} = 89.37$ The value exceeds critical value of $F_{2,50}$ i.e., 3.2, rejecting the hypothesis of no difference in the growth for the two periods.		
Exponential Trend Coefficient	-0.779	0.398	-1.646
t-statistic	-9.92	3.23	-18.99
	Yield		
Linear Trend Coefficient	12.70	6.96	17.46
t-statistic	20.01	7.22	10.29
Chow Test	$S_1 = 274832$; $S_2 = 27782.6$; $S_3 = 157762.9$; $S_4 = 185545.5$; $S_5 = 89286.5$; $F = \frac{(89286.5/2)}{(185545.5/50)} = 12.03$ The value exceeds critical value of $F_{2,50}$ i.e., 3.2, rejecting the hypothesis of no difference in the growth for the two periods.		
Exponential Trend Coefficient	1.793	1.347	2.021
t-statistic	25.39	7.30	10.52
Chow Test	$S_1 = 0.33409$; $S_2 = 0.10049$; $S_3 = 0.19830$; $S_4 = 0.29879$; $S_5 = 0.03530$; $F = \frac{(0.03530/2)}{(0.29879/50)} = 2.95$ The value is less than critical value of $F_{2,50}$ i.e., 3.2, thus not rejecting the hypothesis of no difference in the growth for the two periods.		

Jowar

Jowar is a declining crop (Table 2.6a). Output went up until the mid-seventies and are now back to the early fifties levels. Area under *jowar* was roughly constant until the mid-seventies at around 16 million hectares but has declined substantially since to 9.5 million hectares.

In the first period, jowar output increase is 0.09 million tonnes per year and in the second period, it declines by -0.14 million tonnes (Table 2.6b).

Area grew in the first period but only by 0.01 million hectares whereas it declined by –0.30 million hectares in the second period from

1975-76 to 2003/04. In the overall period, the decline was of -0.15 million hectares per year. Yield growth was 5-6 kgs per hectare annual in the entire period.

Table 2.6a

Area, Production and Yield of Jowar 1950/51 to 2001/2003

(Area in million hectares; Production in million tonnes; Yield in kgs/hec)

	3 YR AVG 1950-1952	3 YR AVG 1974-1976	3 YR AVG 2001-2003
Area	16.34	16.02	9.49
Production	7.17	10.52	7.28
Yield	435	657	767

Table 2.6b

Area, Production and Yield Trends of Jowar 1950/51 to 2003/04

Jowar		*Production*			*Area*			*Yield*		
		1950-51 to 2003-04	*1950-51 to 1974-75*	*1975-76 to 2003-04*	*1950-51 to 2003-04*	*1950-51 to 1974-75*	*1975-76 to 2003-04*	*1950-51 to 2003-04*	*1950-51 to 1974-75*	*1975-76 to 2003-04*
Linear	b	0.03	0.09	-0.14	-0.15	0.01	-0.30	8.87	5.12	6.28
	t	2.23	2.84	-4.34	-11.12	0.43	-14.50	13.31	3.55	3.30
Compound	b	0.37	1.16	-1.46	-1.08	0.65	-2.29	1.47	1.10	0.85
	t	2.23	2.88	-4.68	-10.61	0.41	-13.99	14.04	3.60	3.41

Note: Units as in Table 2.6a; b: annual growth rate; t: t-statistic.

Table 2.6c shows that output and area trends were significantly different in the two periods.

Table 2.6c

Tests of Significance of Growth Rate Differences in the Periods 1950-51 to 1974-75 and 1975-76 to 2003-04

	1950-51 to 2003-04	*1950-51 to 1974-75*	*1975-76 to 2003-04*
	Production		
Linear Trend Coefficient	0.034	0.091	-0.136
t-statistic	2.23	2.84	-4.34
Chow Test	$S_1 = 154.816$; $S_2 = 30.376$; $S_3 = 54.082$; $S_4 = 84.458$; $S_5 = 70.358$; $F = \frac{(70.358/2)}{(84.458/50)} = 20.83$		

contd...

...contd...

	1950-51 to 2003-04	*1950-51 to 1974-75*	*1975-76 to 2003-04*
	The value exceeds critical value of $F_{2,50}$ i.e., 3.2, rejecting the hypothesis of no difference in the growth for the two periods.		
Exponential Trend Coefficient	0.370	1.162	-1.460
t-statistic	2.23	2.88	-4.68
Chow Test	$S_1 = 1.86550;\ S_2 = 0.47995;\ S_3 = 0.54243;\ S_4 = 1.02238;$ $S_5 = 0.84312;\ F = \frac{(0.84312/2)}{(1.02238/50)} = 20.62$		
	The value exceeds critical value of $F_{2,50}$ i.e., 3.2, rejecting the hypothesis of no difference in the growth for the two periods.		
	Area		
Linear Trend Coefficient	-0.151	0.012	-0.299
t-statistic	-11.12	0.43	-14.50
Chow Test	$S_1 = 125.192;\ S_2 = 21.959;\ S_3 = 23.327;\ S_4 = 45.286;$ $S_5 = 79.906;\ F = \frac{(79.906/2)}{(45.286/50)} = 44.11$		
	The value exceeds critical value of $F_{2,50}$ i.e., 3.2, rejecting the hypothesis of no difference in the growth for the two periods.		
Exponential Trend Coefficient	-1.081	0.653	-2.291
t-statistic	-10.61	0.41	-13.99
	Yield		
Linear Trend Coefficient	8.87	5.12	6.28
t-statistic	13.31	3.55	3.30
Chow Test	$S_1 = 303136;\ S_2 = 62307.8;\ S_3 = 198365.7;\ S_4 = 260673.5;$ $S_5 = 42462.5;\ F = \frac{(42462.5/2)}{(260673.5/50)} = 4.07$		
	The value exceeds critical value of $F_{2,50}$ i.e., 3.2, rejecting the hypothesis of no difference in the growth for the two periods.		
Exponential Trend Coefficient	1.466	1.095	0.847
t-statistic	14.04	3.60	3.41
Chow Test	$S_1 = 0.73307;\ S_2 = 0.27429;\ S_3 = 0.33516;$ $S_4 = 0.60945;$ $S_5 = 0.12362;\ F = \frac{(0.12362/2)}{(0.60945/50)} = 5.07$		
	The value exceeds critical value of $F_{2,50}$ i.e., 3.2, thus rejecting the hypothesis of no difference in the growth for the two periods.		

Bajra

Area under *bajra* went up from 9.77 million hectares to 11.23 million hectares in the mid-seventies and the fell back to 9.23 million hectares in the second period (Table 2.7a). Output kept on rising from 2.5 million tonnes to 4.95 million tonnes and is now at 8.7 million tonnes. Output expansion is yield sourced, with yield almost doubling in each period.

Table 2.7a

Area, Production and Yield of Bajra 1950/51 to 2001/2003

(Area in million hectares; Production in million tonnes; Yield in kgs/hec)

	3 YR AVG 1950-1952	3 YR AVG 1974-1976	3 YR AVG 2001-2003
Area	9.77	11.23	9.23
Production	2.50	4.95	8.70
Yield	277	442	874

Linear output growth in the two periods is roughly constant at 0.10-0.11 million tonnes per annum (Table 2.7b). Annual growth of 0.10 million hectares in area under *bajra* in the first period is counterbalanced by an annual decline of -0.09 million hectares in the second period. Yield growth of 6.73 kgs/hec in the first phase, more than doubles at 14.79 kgs/hec in the second phase. Understandably, the compound output growth rate falls in the second period, the area growth rate of 0.85 per cent compound annual in the first phase is counterbalanced by a negative growth rate of 0.84 per cent annual in the second phase, while the yield growth rate goes up from 1.77 per cent annual to 2.39 per cent annual.

Table 2.7b

Area, Production and Yield Trends of Bajra 1950/51 to 2003/04

Bajra		*Production*			*Area*			*Yield*		
		1950-51 to 2003-04	*1950-51 to 1974-75*	*1975-76 to 2003-04*	*1950-51 to 2003-04*	*1950-51 to 1974-75*	*1975-76 to 2003-04*	*1950-51 to 2003-04*	*1950-51 to 1974-75*	*1975-76 to 2003-04*
Linear	b	0.08	0.11	0.10	-0.04	0.10	-0.09	9.76	6.73	14.79
	t	6.95	3.86	2.87	-3.94	4.61	-5.11	10.17	3.43	5.18
Compound	b	1.63	2.63	1.53	-0.34	0.85	-0.84	1.98	1.77	2.39
	t	7.70	4.32	2.66	-4.01	4.60	-4.99	11.74	3.64	5.14

Note: Units as in Table 2.7a; b: annual growth rate; t: t-statistic.

Output growth rate estimates are not significantly different between the two periods for *bajra* (Table 2.7c). Area growth rates are significant. The compound growth rate of yield is significantly different but the linear estimate is not.

Table 2.7c

Tests of Significance of Growth Rate Differences in the Periods 1950-51 to 1974-75 and 1975-76 to 2003-04

	1950-51 to 2003-04	*1950-51 to 1974-75*	*1975-76 to 2003-04*
	Production		
Linear Trend Coefficient	0.084	0.114	0.104
t-statistic	6.95	3.86	2.87
Chow Test	$S_1 = 100.2118;\ S_2 = 25.947;\ S_3 = 71.714;\ S_4 = 97.661;$ $S_5 = 2.5502;\ F = \frac{(2.5502/2)}{(97.661/50)} = 0.65$		
	The value is less than critical value of $F_{2,50}$ i.e., 3.2, not rejecting the hypothesis of no difference in the growth for the two periods.		
Exponential Trend Coefficient	1.628	2.626	1.528
t-statistic	7.70	4.32	2.66
Chow Test	$S_1 = 2.99783;\ S_2 = 1.08004;\ S_3 = 1.77984;\ S_4 = 2.85984;$ $S_5 = 0.13799;\ F = \frac{(0.13799/2)}{(2.85984/50)} = 1.21$		
	The value is less than critical value of $F_{2,50}$ i.e., 3.2, not rejecting the hypothesis of no difference in the growth for the two periods.		
	Area		
Linear Trend Coefficient	-0.036	0.095	-0.085
t-statistic	-3.94	4.61	-5.11
Chow Test	$S_1 = 55.507;\ S_2 = 12.683;\ S_3 = 15.221;\ S_4 = 27.904;$ $S_5 = 27.603;\ F = \frac{(27.603/2)}{(27.904/50)} = 24.73$		
	The value exceeds critical value of $F_{2,50}$ i.e., 3.2, rejecting the hypothesis of no difference in the growth for the two periods.		
Exponential Trend Coefficient	-0.339	0.845	-0.836
t-statistic	-4.01	4.60	-4.99

contd...

contd...

	1950-51 to 2003-04	1950-51 to 1974-75	1975-76 to 2003-04
	Yield		
Linear Trend Coefficient	9.76	6.73	14.79
t-statistic	10.17	3.43	5.18
Chow Test	$S_1 = 628480;\ S_2 = 115109.1;\ S_3 = 446019.2;\ S_4 = 561128.3;$ $S_5 = 67351.7;\ F = \frac{(67351.7/2)}{(561128.3/50)} = 3.00$ The value is less than critical value of $F_{2,50}$ i.e., 3.2, not rejecting the hypothesis of no difference in the growth for the two periods.		
Exponential Trend Coefficient	1.975	1.773	2.386
t-statistic	11.74	3.64	5.14
Chow Test	$S_1 = 1.89349;\ S_2 = 0.6980;\ S_3 = 1.1544;\ S_4 = 1.8524;$ $S_5 = 0.04109;\ F = \frac{(0.04109/2)}{(1.8524/50)} = 0.55$ The value is less than critical value of $F_{2,50}$ i.e., 3.2, thus not rejecting the hypothesis of no difference in the growth for the two periods.		

Maize

Maize is a crop in which there has been output and productivity growth throughout the period. Maize is not only consumed as a staple but is also important as poultry feed and as an input for the starch industry, and use for these non-food/agricultural activities has been expanding. Yield went up from around 5 quintals per hectare to around a tonne in the period from 1950/51 to 1975/76. It further grew from 1.08 tonnes/hec in 1975/76 to 1.79 tonnes/hec by 2003/04. Area expansion was negligible in the second period (Table 2.8a), in which output almost doubled from 6.41 million tonnes to 11.31 million tonnes.

Table 2.8a

All India Area, Production and Yield of Maize from 1950-51 to 2001-2003

Area in million hectares; Production in million tonnes; Yield in kgs/hec

	3 YR AVG 1950-1952	3 YR AVG 1974-1976	3 YR AVG 2001-2003
Area	3.24	5.95	6.32
Production	1.91	6.41	11.31
Yield	587.00	1075.50	1791.00

The absolute growth in output at an annual level of 1.03 lakh tonnes in the period 1950/51-1974/75 decreases to an annual rate of 0.25 lakh tonnes in the period 1975/76 to 2003/04 and the annual compound growth rate from 4.73 per cent to 2.86 per cent (Table 2.8b). The productivity growth rate goes up from 2.02 per cent compound annual to 2.34 per cent annual and the growth rate of area declines from 2.67 per cent to 0.52 per cent compound annual.

Table 2.8b

Area, Production and Yield Trends of Maize 1950/51 to 2003/04

Maize		*Production*			*Area*			*Yield*		
		1950-51 to 2003-04	*1950-51 to 1974-75*	*1975-76 to 2003-04*	*1950-51 to 2003-04*	*1950-51 to 1974-75*	*1975-76 to 2003-04*	*1950-51 to 2003-04*	*1950-51 to 1974-75*	*1975-76 to 2003-04*
Linear	b	0.18	1.03	0.25	0.06	0.12	0.03	21.76	17.01	33.26
	t	21.38	11.94	10.96	15.02	23.31	5.88	18.10	6.17	11.84
Compound	b	2.97	4.73	2.86	1.11	2.67	0.52	1.84	2.02	2.34
	t	21.91	11.98	11.19	13.50	23.37	6.00	19.47	6.28	11.27

Note: Units as in Table 2.8a; b: annual growth rate; t: t-statistic.

Table 2.8c shows that area, production and yield growth rates are significantly different in the two period.

Table 2.8c

Tests of Significance of Growth Rate Differences in the Periods 1950-51 to 1974-75 and 1975-76 to 2003-04

	1950-51 to 2003-04	*1950-51 to 1974-75*	*1975-76 to 2003-04*
	Production		
Linear Trend Coefficient	0.181	0.184	0.253
t-statistic	21.38	11.94	10.96
Chow Test	$S_1 = 49.1026;\ S_2 = 7.0823;\ S_3 = 29.2588;\ S_4 = 36.3411;$ $S_5 = 12.7615;\ F = \frac{(12.7615/2)}{(36.3411/50)} = 8.78$		
	The value exceds critical value of $F_{2,50}$ i.e., 3.2, rejecting the hypothesis of no difference in the growth for the two periods.		
Exponential Trend Coefficient	2.965	4.734	2.855
t-statistic	21.91	11.98	11.19

contd...

...contd...

	1950-51 to 2003-04	1950-51 to 1974-75	1975-76 to 2003-04
Chow Test	$S_1 = 1.2134$; $S_2 = 0.4459$; $S_3 = 0.3470$; $S_4 = 0.7929$; $S_5 = 0.4205$; $F = \frac{(0.4205/2)}{(0.7929/50)} = 13.25$ The value exceeds critical value of $F_{2,50}$ i.e., 3.2, rejecting the hypothesis of no difference in the growth for the two periods.		
	Area		
Linear Trend Coefficient	0.055	0.121	0.032
t-statistic	15.02	23.31	5.88
Chow Test	$S_1 = 9.2503$; $S_2 = 0.8021$; $S_3 = 1.6767$; $S_4 = 2.4788$; $S_5 = 6.7715$; $F = \frac{(6.7715/2)}{(2.4788/50)} = 68.29$ The value exceeds critical value of $F_{2,50}$ i.e., 3.2, rejecting the hypothesis of no difference in the growth for the two periods.		
Exponential Trend Coefficient	1.112	2.665	0.521
t-statistic	13.50	23.37	6.00
	Yield		
Linear Trend Coefficient	21.76	17.01	33.26
t-statistic	18.10	6.17	11.84
Chow Test	$S_1 = 986964.9$; $S_2 = 227209.3$; $S_3 = 432402.4$; $S_4 = 659611.7$; $S_5 = 327353.2$; $F = \frac{(327353.2/2)}{(659611.7/50)} = 12.41$ The value exceeds critical value of $F_{2,50}$ i.e., 3.2, rejecting the hypothesis of no difference in the growth for the two periods.		
Exponential Trend Coefficient	1.844	2.017	2.343
t-statistic	19.47	6.28	11.27
Chow Test	$S_1 = 0.6010$; $S_2 = 0.3023$; $S_3 = 0.2316$; $S_4 = 0.5339$; $S_5 = 0.0671$; $F = \frac{(0.0671/2)}{(0.5339/50)} = 3.14$ The value is less than critical value of $F_{2,50}$ i.e., 3.2, thus not rejecting the hypothesis of no difference in the growth for the two periods.		

Pulses

Area under pulses rises from around 19 million hectares to 23 lakh hectares in the first phase and then stagnates. The output expansion in the second phase is sourced from yield. Output rises from 8.42 million tones to 11.53 million tonnes in the first phase and then the growth slows down and it is at 13.15 million tonnes by now (Table 2.9a).

Table 2.9a

All India Production, Area and Yield of Pulses 1950/51-2001/2003

Area in million hectares; Production in million tonnes; Yield in kgs/hec

	3 YR AVG 1950-1952	3 YR AVG 1974-1976	3 YR AVG 2001-2003
Area	18.94	23.24	22.65
Production	8.42	11.53	13.15
Yield	444.50	494.00	596.00

The annual increase in production was low going up from 3000 tonnes in the first period to 8000 tonnes in the second phase, the compound annual growth rate rising from 0.32 per cent to 0.63 per cent (Table 2.9b). Area growth declines from a figure of 0.27 per cent annual in the period 1950/51 to 1974/75 to minus 0.28 per cent annual in the second period. Yield growth in the second phase was, therefore, at 0.91 per cent annual.

Table 2.9b

Area, Production and Yield Trends of Pulses 1950/51 to 2003/04

Pulses		*Production*			*Area*			*Yield*		
		1950-51 to 2003-04	*1950-51 to 1974-75*	*1975-76 to 2003-04*	*1950-51 to 2003-04*	*1950-51 to 1974-75*	*1975-76 to 2003-04*	*1950-51 to 2003-04*	*1950-51 to 1974-75*	*1975-76 to 2003-04*
Linear	b	0.06	0.03	0.08	0.01	0.01	-0.06	2.78	0.29	4.86
	t	5.69	0.79	2.74	0.43	1.26	-2.98	7.15	0.24	5.49
Compound	b	0.56	0.32	0.63	0.03	0.27	-0.28	0.53	0.05	0.91
	t	5.52	0.90	2.64	0.54	1.37	-3.00	6.74	0.18	5.21

Note: Units as in Table 2.9a; b: annual growth rate; t: t-statistic.

Table 2.9c shows that there is no significant difference in the growth rate experience of the two phases but the area and yield growth experience is different, with land being diverted from pulses and productivity going up marginally.

Table 2.9c

Tests of Significance of Growth Rate Differences in the Periods 1950-51 to 1974-75 and 1975-76 to 2003-04

	1950-51 to 2003-04	1950-51 to 1974-75	1975-76 to 2003-04
	Production		
Linear Trend Coefficient	0.064	0.030	0.077
t-statistic	5.69	0.79	2.74
Chow Test	$S_1 = 87.496$; $S_2 = 42.207$; $S_3 = 43.362$; $S_4 = 85.569$; $S_5 = 1.927$; $F = \frac{(1.927/2)}{(85.569/50)} = 0.56$		
	The value is less than critical value of $F_{2,50}$ i.e., 3.2, not rejecting the hypothesis of no difference in the growth for the two periods.		
Exponential Trend Coefficient	0.561	0.323	0.627
t-statistic	5.52	0.90	2.64
Chow Test	$S_1 = 0.6998$; $S_2 = 0.3830$; $S_3 = 0.3083$; $S_4 = 0.6913$; $S_5 = 0.0085$; $F = \frac{(0.0085/2)}{(0.6913/50)} = 0.31$		
	The value is less than critical value of $F_{2,50}$ i.e., 3.2, not rejecting the hypothesis of no difference in the growth for the two periods.		
	Area		
Linear Trend Coefficient	0.005	0.055	-0.062
t-statistic	0.43	1.26	-2.98
Chow Test	$S_1 = 93.927$; $S_2 = 57.130$; $S_3 = 23.872$; $S_4 = 81.002$; $S_5 = 12.925$; $F = \frac{(12.925/2)}{(81.002/50)} = 3.99$		
	The value exceeds critical value of $F_{2,50}$ i.e., 3.2, rejecting the hypothesis of no difference in the growth for the two periods.		
Exponential Trend Coefficient	0.029	0.274	-0.278
t-statistic	0.54	1.37	-3.00
	Yield		
Linear Trend Coefficient	2.78	0.291	4.864
t-statistic	7.15	0.24	5.49
Chow Test	$S_1 = 103296$; $S_2 = 43238.3$; $S_3 = 43089.2$; $S_4 = 86327.5$; $S_5 = 16970.5$; $F = \frac{(16970.5/2)}{(86327.5/50)} = 4.91$		

contd...

...contd...

	1950-51 to 2003-04	1950-51 to 1974-75	1975-76 to 2003-04
	The value exceeds critical value of $F_{2,50}$ i.e., 3.2, rejecting the hypothesis of no difference in the growth for the two periods.		
Exponential Trend Coefficient	0.531	0.048	0.906
t-statistic	6.74	0.18	5.21
Chow Test	$S_1 = 0.4216;\ S_2 = 0.1992;\ S_3 = 0.1640;\ S_4 = 0.3632;$ $S_5 = 0.0584;\ F = \frac{(0.0584/2)}{(0.3632/50)} = 4.02$		
	The value exceeds critical value of $F_{2,50}$ i.e., 3.2, rejecting the hypothesis of no difference in the growth for the two periods.		

Gram

Gram is a very popular pulse in India but as Table 2.10a shows area under it ranging at around 7.77 million hectares, went down to 6.15 million hectares in the recent period. Output growth was yield based.

Table 2.10a

All India Area Production and Yield of Gram

Area in million hectares; Production in million tonnes; Yield in kgs/hec

	3 YR AVG 1950-1952	3 YR AVG 1974-1976	3 YR AVG 2001/2003
Area	7.22	7.77	6.15
Production	3.75	4.77	5.17
Yield	506	652	791

Table 2.10b shows that production growth was negative in the period 1950/1975 and only 13000 tonnes annual in the period 1975/2004. Area growth was negative at 5000 hectares annual in the two periods and the yield growth 2.7 kgs/hec went up to 6.39 kgs in the second period. The annual compound area decline of -0.54 per cent goes up to -0.66 per cent annual decline in the second period, in which the productivity growth is 0.9 per cent annual.

Table 2.10c verifies the dismal story of gram in India. Estimates of growth are not statistically different in the two periods.

Table 2.10b

Area, Production and Yield Trends of Gram 1950/51 to 2003/04

Gram		Production			Area			Yield		
		1950-51 to 2003-04	1950-51 to 1974-75	1975-76 to 2003-04	1950-51 to 2003-04	1950-51 to 1974-75	1975-76 to 2003-04	1950-51 to 2003-04	1950-51 to 1974-75	1975-76 to 2003-04
Linear	b	0.002	-0.008	0.013	-0.05	-0.05	-0.05	4.75	2.70	6.39
	t	0.24	-0.31	0.67	-6.75	-1.65	-2.74	7.83	1.31	4.45
Compound	b	0.05	-0.09	0.24	-0.67	-0.54	-0.66	0.72	0.05	0.90
	t	0.33	-0.16	0.63	-6.76	-1.59	-2.74	7.41	1.27	4.20

Note: Units as in Table 2.10a; b: annual growth rate; t: t-statistic.

Table 2.10c

Tests of Significance of Growth Rate Differences in the Periods 1950-51 to 1974-75 and 1975-76 to 2003-04

	1950-51 to 2003-04	1950-51 to 1974-75	1975-76 to 2003-04
	Production		
Linear Trend Coefficient	0.002	-0.008	0.013
t-statistic	0.24	-0.31	0.67
Chow Test	$S_1 = 40.500;\ S_2 = 20.963;\ S_3 = 19.161;\ S_4 = 40.124;$ $S_5 = 0.376;\ F = \frac{(0.376/2)}{(40.124/50)} = 0.23$ The value is less than critical value of $F_{2,50}$ i.e., 3.2, not rejecting the hypothesis of no difference in the growth for the two periods.		
Exponential Trend Coefficient	0.053	-0.087	0.239
t-statistic	0.33	-0.16	0.63
Chow Test	$S_1 = 1.6856;\ S_2 = 0.8752;\ S_3 = 0.8004;\ S_4 = 1.6756;$ $S_5 = 0.0100;\ F = \frac{(0.0100/2)}{(0.6756/50)} = 0.15$ The value is less than critical value of $F_{2,50}$ i.e., 3.2, not rejecting the hypothesis of no difference in the growth for the two periods.		
	Area		
Linear Trend Coefficient	-0.051	-0.047	-0.045
t-statistic	-6.75	-1.65	-2.74
Chow Test	$S_1 = 39.240;\ S_2 = 24.189;\ S_3 = 14.920;\ S_4 = 39.109;$ $S_5 = 0.131;\ F = \frac{(0.131/2)}{(39.109/50)} = 0.08$		

contd...

...contd...

	1950-51 to 2003-04	*1950-51 to 1974-75*	*1975-76 to 2003-04*
	The value is less than critical value of $F_{2,50}$ i.e., 3.2, not rejecting the hypothesis of no difference in the growth for the two periods.		
Exponential Trend Coefficient	-0.667	-0.538	-0.663
t-statistic	-6.76	-1.59	-2.74
	Yield		
Linear Trend Coefficient	4.75	2.70	6.39
t-statistic	7.83	1.31	4.45
Chow Test	$S_1 = 250973.9;\ S_2 = 127220.6;\ S_3 = 112805.2;\ S_4 = 240025.8;$ $S_5 = 10948.1;\ F = \frac{(10948.1/2)}{(240025.8/50)} = 1.14$		
	The value is less than critical value of $F_{2,50}$ i.e., 3.2, not rejecting the hypothesis of no difference in the growth for the two periods.		
Exponential Trend Coefficient	0.724	0.045	0.909
t-statistic	7.41	1.27	4.20
Chow Test	$S_1 = 0.6463;\ S_2 = 0.3762;\ S_3 = 0.2537;\ S_4 = 0.6299;$ $S_5 = 0.0164;\ F = \frac{(0.0164/2)}{(0.6299/50)} = 0.65$		
	The value is less than critical value of $F_{2,50}$ i.e., 3.2, not rejecting the hypothesis of no difference in the growth for the two periods.		

Tur

The more general pulses trend is shown more vividly in the case of *tur*, a favourite of the Indian household menu. Output levels stay at around 1.8 to 2 lakh tonnes in the first phase but rise to 2.27 lakh tonnes in the second phase (Table 2.11a). The underlying demand trend is strong and since yield remains at around seven to seven and a half quintals per hectare, area goes up initially from 2.3 lakh hectares to 2.6 lakh hectares and then to 3.4 lakh hectares.

Output growth at minus 0.02 per cent annual in the first phase goes up to 0.73 per cent annual in the second phase (Table 2.11b). For the whole period the production growth rate is 0.89 per cent annual. Yield growth is negative in all periods. Area growth goes up from 0.47 per cent annual in the first phase to 1.07 per cent annual in the second phase, although all that this means is that on an average the annual growth of area in the first phase of around three hundred hectares goes up to two thousand hectares in the second phase.

Table 2.11a

All India Area Production and Yield of Tur

Area in million hectares; Production in million tonnes; Yield in kgs/hec

	3 YR AVG 1950-1952	3 YR AVG 1974-1976	3 YR AVG 2002-2003
Area	2.32	2.60	3.41
Production	1.78	1.97	2.27
Yield	768	756	667

Table 2.11b

Area, Production and Yield Trends of Tur 1950/51 to 2003/04

Tur		Production			Area			Yield		
		1950-51 to 2003-04	1950-51 to 1974-75	1975-76 to 2003-04	1950-51 to 2003-04	1950-51 to 1974-75	1975-76 to 2003-04	1950-51 to 2003-04	1950-51 to 1974-75	1975-76 to 2003-04
Linear	b	0.02	-0.003	0.02	0.03	0.01	0.03	-0.52	-4.40	-2.23
	t	7.47	-0.47	2.54	17.48	4.33	7.39	-0.72	-1.66	-1.52
Compound	b	0.89	-0.20	0.73	0.95	0.47	1.07	-0.06	-0.66	-0.33
	t	7.12	-0.52	2.66	18.46	4.31	7.46	-0.57	-1.60	-1.56

Note: Units as in Table 2.11a; b: annual growth rate; t: t-statistic.

Growth estimates are significantly different in the two periods (Table 2.11c).

Table 2.11c

Tests of Significance of Growth Rate Differences in the Periods 1950-51 to 1974-75 and 1975-76 to 2003-04

	1950-51 to 2003-04	1950-51 to 1974-75	1975-76 to 2003-04
	Production		
Linear Trend Coefficient	0.018	-0.003	0.016
t-statistic	7.47	-0.47	2.54
Chow Test	$S_1 = 3.9150$; $S_2 = 1.1328$; $S_3 = 2.1122$; $S_4 = 3.2450$; $S_5 = 0.6700$; $F = \frac{(0.6700/2)}{(3.2450/50)} = 5.16$		

contd...

...contd...

	1950-51 to 2003-04	*1950-51 to 1974-75*	*1975-76 to 2003-04*
	The value exceeds critical value of $F_{2,50}$ i.e., 3.2, rejecting the hypothesis of no difference in the growth for the two periods.		
Exponential Trend Coefficient	0.889	-0.201	0.734
t-statistic	7.12	-0.52	2.66
Chow Test	$S_1 = 1.0539;\ S_2 = 0.4514;\ S_3 = 0.4136;\ S_4 = 0.8650;$ $S_5 = 0.1889;\ F = \frac{(0.1889/2)}{(0.8650/50)} = 5.46$		
	The value exceeds critical value of $F_{2,50}$ i.e., 3.2, rejecting the hypothesis of no difference in the growth for the two periods.		
	Area		
Linear Trend Coefficient	0.027	0.011	0.033
t-statistic	17.48	4.33	7.39
Chow Test	$S_1 = 1.6784;\ S_2 = 0.2082;\ S_3 = 1.0706;\ S_4 = 1.2788;$ $S_5 = 0.3996;\ F = \frac{(0.3996/2)}{(1.2788/50)} = 7.81$		
	The value exceeds critical value of $F_{2,50}$ i.e., 3.2, rejecting the hypothesis of no difference in the growth for the two periods.		
Exponential Trend Coefficient	0.952	0.466	1.066
t-statistic	18.46	4.31	7.46
	Yield		
Linear Trend Coefficient	-0.52	-4.40	-2.23
t-statistic	-0.72	-1.66	-1.52
Chow Test	$S_1 = 362028.8;\ S_2 = 211139.6;\ S_3 = 118021.7;\ S_4 = 329161.3;$ $S_5 = 32867.5;\ F = \frac{(32867.5/2)}{(329161.3/50)} = 2.50$		
	The value is less than critical value of $F_{2,50}$ i.e., 3.2, not rejecting the hypothesis of no difference in the growth for the two periods.		
Exponential Trend Coefficient	-0.062	-0.656	-0.330
t-statistic	-0.57	-1.60	-1.56
Chow Test	$S_1 = 0.8286;\ S_2 = 0.5046;\ S_3 = 0.2456;\ S_4 = 0.7502;$ $S_5 = 0.0784;\ F = \frac{(0.0784/2)}{(0.7502/50)} = 2.61$		
	The value is less than critical value of $F_{2,50}$ i.e., 3.2, not rejecting the hypothesis of no difference in the growth for the two periods.		

Nine Oilseeds

Oilseeds are important crops of the Indian agricultural economy. They are, in fact, prominent in the rainfed and dry land areas, and for a long period irrigated area under oilseeds was marginal and is still low. Area under oilseeds has expanded, in some areas at the expense of grain crops, for example sunflower or mustard in *rabi* in north India and groundnut in Gujarat, Maharashtra and Andhra Pradesh, in others by cropping on earlier fallows, for example soya farming in *kharif* fallows in Madhya Pradesh and in yet others with increase in cropping intensity with irrigation, particularly in areas where water deltas are low. Table 2.12a shows that area under oilseeds goes up by around 35 to 50 per cent in the two phases. In the first phase, with area going up from 11.2 million hectares to 17.1 million hectares and yield going up marginally from 4.56 quintals per hectare to 5.78 quintals, output goes up from 5.1 million tonnes to 9.88 million tonnes. In the second phase, in addition to the area expansion, yield rises rapidly from 5.78 quintals to 8.9 quintals per hectare and output also goes up from 9.88 million tonnes to 20.26 million tonnes.

Table 2.12a

All India Production, Area and Yield of Oilseeds Triennium Averages

Area in million hectares; Production in million tonnes; Yield in kgs/hec

	3 YR AVG 1950-1952	*3 YR AVG 1974-1976*	*3 YR AVG 2001-03*
Area	11.21	17.12	22.37
Production	5.10	9.88	20.26
Yield	456	578	890

Output growth rate goes up from 2.3 per cent annual to 3.7 per cent annual from 1950/1975 to 1975/2003. This is sourced by area growth remaining at 1.76 per cent annual in the first phase and 1.65 per cent annual in the second phase. In the second phase, yield growth increases from 0.43 per cent annual in the first phase to 2.06 per cent annual (Table 2.12b). Yield growth, therefore, expands four times from the first phase and in the second phase, area and yield are almost equal sources of growth.

Table 2.12b

Area, Production and Yield Trends of Nine Oilseeds 1950/51 to 2003/04

Nine Oilseeds		Production			Area			Yield		
		1950-51 to 2003-04	1950-51 to 1974-75	1975-76 to 2003-04	1950-51 to 2003-04	1950-51 to 1974-75	1975-76 to 2003-04	1950-51 to 2003-04	1950-51 to 1974-75	1975-76 to 2003-04
Linear	b	0.35	0.16	0.56	0.28	0.26	0.34	8.86	2.15	14.68
	t	15.29	7.55	8.90	19.99	14.60	7.28	12.73	1.82	8.60
Compound	b	3.01	2.30	3.75	1.60	1.86	1.65	1.38	0.43	2.06
	t	21.85	7.80	9.43	23.94	14.05	7.82	13.77	1.76	8.81

Note: Units as in Table 2.12a; b: annual growth rate; t: t-statistic.

Apart from area which grew in both periods, yield and output growth estimates are significantly different in the two phases (Table 2.12c).

Table 2.12c

Tests of Significance of Growth Rate Differences in the Periods 1950-51 to 1974-75 and 1975-76 to 2003-04

	1950-51 to 2003-04	1950-51 to 1974-75	1975-76 to 2003-04
	Production		
Linear Trend Coefficient	0.352	0.157	0.555
t-statistic	15.29	7.55	8.90
Chow Test	$S_1 = 362.241$; $S_2 = 12.997$; $S_3 = 213.561$; $S_4 = 226.558$; $S_5 = 135.673$; $F = \frac{(135.673/2)}{(226.558/50)} = 14.97$		
	The value exceeds critical value of $F_{2,50}$ i.e., 3.2, rejecting the hypothesis of no difference in the growth for the two periods.		
Exponential Trend Coefficient	3.008	2.295	3.745
t-statistic	21.85	7.80	9.43
Chow Test	$S_1 = 1.2556$; $S_2 = 0.2534$; $S_3 = 0.8334$; $S_4 = 1.0868$; $S_5 = 0.1688$; $F = \frac{(0.1688/2)}{(1.0868/50)} = 3.88$		
	The value exceeds critical value of $F_{2,50}$ i.e., 3.2, rejecting the hypothesis of no difference in the growth for the two periods.		

contd...

...contd...

	1950-51 to 2003-04	1950-51 to 1974-75	1975-76 to 2003-04
	Area		
Linear Trend Coefficient	0.283	0.256	0.340
t-statistic	19.99	14.60	7.28
Chow Test	$S_1 = 137.065;\ S_2 = 9.186;\ S_3 = 119.662;\ S_4 = 128.848;$ $S_5 = 8.217;\ F = \frac{(8.217/2)}{(128.848/50)} = 1.59$ The value is less than critical value of $F_{2,50}$ i.e., 3.2, not rejecting the hypothesis of no difference in the growth for the two periods.		
Exponential Trend Coefficient	1.603	1.864	1.645
t-statistic	23.94	14.05	7.82
	Yield		
Linear Trend Coefficient	8.856	2.145	14.68
t-statistic	12.73	1.82	8.60
Chow Test	$S_1 = 330069.7;\ S_2 = 41643.0;\ S_3 = 159943.9;\ S_4 = 201586.9;$ $S_5 = 128482.8;\ F = \frac{(128482.8/2)}{(201586.9/50)} = 15.93$ The value exceeds critical value of $F_{2,50}$ i.e., 3.2, rejecting the hypothesis of no difference in the growth for the two periods.		
Exponential Trend Coefficient	1.380	0.426	2.061
t-statistic	13.77	1.76	8.81
Chow Test	$S_1 = 0.6751;\ S_2 = 0.1737;\ S_3 = 0.2940;\ S_4 = 0.4677;$ $S_5 = 0.2074;\ F = \frac{(0.2074/2)}{(0.4677/50)} = 11.09$ The value exceeds critical value of $F_{2,50}$ i.e., 3.2, rejecting the hypothesis of no difference in the growth for the two periods.		

Groundnut

Area under groundnut increases from 4.71 million hectares in 1950/1952 to 7.14 million hectares in 1974/1976. It then falls to 6.06 million hectares until 2001/2003 (Table 2.13a). Yield increases at a slow pace in the first period from 7.1 quintals per hectare to 8.3 quintals/hec. It then goes up to over a tonne, at 10.62 quintals per hectare in 2001/2003. Groundnut production increases from 3.34 million tones in 1950/1952 to 5.94 million tonnes in 1974/1976 and is placed at 6.44 million tonnes in 2001/2003.

Table 2.13a

All India Production, Area and Yield of Groundnut Triennium Averages

Area in million hectares; Production in million tonnes; Yield in kgs/hec

	3 YR AVG 1950-1952	3 YR AVG 1974-1976	3 YR AVG 2001-2003
Area	4.71	7.14	6.06
Production	3.34	5.94	6.44
Yield	712	829	1062

Output growth rate declines in the second period from 2.01 per cent compound annual in the period 1950/51-1974/75 to 0.69 per cent annual in the period 1975/76-2003/04 (Table 2.13b). Area growth declines from 2.06 per cent compound annual in the first time period to minus 0.26 per cent annual in the second period. Meanwhile, yield growth in the second period at 0.96 per cent compound annual is higher than minus 0.04 per cent annual in the first period. Groundnut is definitely giving way to other crops in the second period.

Table 2.13b

Area, Production and Yield Trends of Groundnut 1950/51 to 2003/04

Groundnut		Production			Area			Yield		
		1950-51 to 2003-04	1950-51 to 1974-75	1975-76 to 2003-04	1950-51 to 2003-04	1950-51 to 1974-75	1975-76 to 2003-04	1950-51 to 2003-04	1950-51 to 1974-75	1975-76 to 2003-04
Linear	b	0.08	0.09	0.05	0.03	0.12	-0.02	7.03	-0.09	9.63
	t	8.24	4.94	1.76	4.63	7.90	-1.00	6.55	-0.04	3.06
Compound	b	1.34	2.01	0.69	0.54	2.06	-0.26	0.80	-0.04	0.96
	t	8.47	5.02	1.55	4.71	7.60	-1.19	6.41	-0.12	2.85

Note: Units as in Table 2.13a; b: annual growth rate; t: t-statistic.

Table 2.13c estimates systematic and significant differences in growth estimates between the two periods, apart from compound output growth which is low in both periods.

Table 2.13c

Tests of Significance of Growth Rate Differences in the Periods 1950-51 to 1974-75 and 1975-76 to 2003-04

	1950-51 to 2003-04	1950-51 to 1974-75	1975-76 to 2003-04
	Production		
Linear Trend Coefficient	0.076	0.088	0.051
t-statistic	8.24	4.94	1.76
Chow Test	$S_1 = 57.425;\ S_2 = 9.590;\ S_3 = 46.312;\ S_4 = 55.902;$ $S_5 = 1.523;\ F = \frac{(1.523/2)}{(55.902/50)} = 0.68$		
	The value is less than critical value of $F_{2,50}$ i.e., 3.2, not rejecting the hypothesis of no difference in the growth for the two periods.		
Exponential Trend Coefficient	1.343	2.011	0.691
t-statistic	8.47	5.02	1.55
Chow Test	$S_1 = 1.6898;\ S_2 = 0.4697;\ S_3 = 1.0773;\ S_4 = 1.5470;$ $S_5 = 0.1428;\ F = \frac{(0.1428/2)}{(1.5470/50)} = 2.31$		
	The value is less than critical value of $F_{2,50}$ i.e., 3.2, not rejecting the hypothesis of no difference in the growth for the two periods.		
	Area		
Linear Trend Coefficient	0.034	0.122	-0.016
t-statistic	4.63	7.90	-1.00
Chow Test	$S_1 = 36.662;\ S_2 = 7.114;\ S_3 = 14.385;\ S_4 = 21.499;$ $S_5 = 15.163;\ F = \frac{(15.163/2)}{(21.499/50)} = 17.63$		
	The value exceeds critical value of $F_{2,50}$ i.e., 3.2, rejecting the hypothesis of no difference in the growth for the two periods.		
Exponential Trend Coefficient	0.543	2.059	-0.261
t-statistic	4.71	7.60	-1.19
	Yield		
Linear Trend Coefficient	7.030	-0.092	9.628
t-statistic	6.55	-0.04	3.06
Chow Test	$S_1 = 785027;\ S_2 = 161504.9;\ S_3 = 542264.4;\ S_4 = 703769.3;$ $S_5 = 81257.7;\ F = \frac{(81257.7/2)}{(703769.3/50)} = 2.89$		

contd...

...contd...

	1950-51 to 2003-04	1950-51 to 1974-75	1975-76 to 2003-04
	The value is less than critical value of $F_{2,50}$ i.e., 3.2, not rejecting the hypothesis of no difference in the growth for the two periods.		
Exponential Trend Coefficient	0.797	-0.040	0.957
t-statistic	6.41	-0.12	2.85
Chow Test	$S_1 = 1.0458;\ S_2 = 0.3303;\ S_3 = 0.6140;\ S_4 = 0.9443;$ $S_5 = 0.1015;\ F = \frac{(0.1015/2)}{(0.9443/50)} = 2.69$		
	The value is less than critical value of $F_{2,50}$ i.e., 3.2, not rejecting the hypothesis of no difference in the growth for the two periods.		

Rapeseed and Mustard

Rapeseed and mustard is the rising crop in the oilseed sector. Output grows up from 0.85 million tonnes in 1950/1952 to 2.1 million tonnes in 1974/1976 and further to 4.99 million tonnes in 2001/2003 (Table 2.14a). Area goes up from 2.24 million hectares in 1950/1952 to 3.51 million hectares in 1974/1976 and then more than doubles at 5 million hectares in 2001/2003. Yield growth is also sourced by yield expansion from 3.8 quintals in 1950/1952 to 5.96 quintals in 1974/1976 and then a much higher increase to over a tonne, 10.31 quintals, in 2001/2003.

Table 2.14a

All India Production, Area and Yield of Mustard, Triennium Averages

Area in million hectares; Production in million tonnes; Yield in kgs/hec

	3 YR AVG 1950-1952	3 YR AVG 1974-1976	3 YR AVG 2001-2003
Area	2.24	3.51	5.00
Production	0.85	2.10	4.99
Yield	380	596	1031

In term of growth rates there is a near doubling factor in yield and output determining the growth trajectory. Area growth increases from 2.08 per cent compound annual in the first phase to 2.24 per cent annual in the second phase and yield growth increases from 1.49 per cent compound annual to 2.75 per cent compound annual (Table 2.14b). Output growth, therefore, increases from 3.6 per cent compound annual in the period 1950/51-1975/76 to 5.04 per cent compound annual in 1975/76 to 2003-04.

Table 2.14b

Area, Production and Yield Trends of Rapeseed and Mustard 1950/51 to 2003/04

Rapeseed and Mustard		*Production*			*Area*			*Yield*		
		1950-51 to 2003-04	*1950-51 to 1974-75*	*1975-76 to 2003-04*	*1950-51 to 2003-04*	*1950-51 to 1974-75*	*1975-76 to 2003-04*	*1950-51 to 2003-04*	*1950-51 to 1974-75*	*1975-76 to 2003-04*
Linear	b	0.10	0.05	0.17	0.08	0.06	0.10	12.74	6.82	19.53
	t	14.60	8.97	8.57	14.03	12.10	5.64	15.45	4.39	9.17
Compound	b	4.12	3.60	5.04	2.00	2.08	2.24	2.07	1.49	2.75
	t	23.27	10.10	9.47	18.23	11.71	6.20	16.71	4.12	8.86

Note: Units as in Table 2.14a; b: annual growth rate; t: t-statistic.

Table 2.14c shows that the growth estimates are largely statistically significantly different in the two periods.

Table 2.14c

Tests of Significance of Growth Rate Differences in the Periods 1950-51 to 1974-75 and 1975-76 to 2003-04

	1950-51 to 2003-04	*1950-51 to 1974-75*	*1975-76 to 2003-04*
	Production		
Linear Trend Coefficient	0.103	0.046	0.166
t-statistic	14.60	8.97	8.57
Chow Test	$S_1 = 33.9224;\ S_2 = 0.7796;\ S_3 = 20.5372;$ $S_4 = 21.3168;$ $S_5 = 12.6058;\ F = \frac{(12.6058/2)}{(21.3168/50)} = 14.78$		
	The value exceeds critical value of $F_{2,50}$ i.e., 3.2, rejecting the hypothesis of no difference in the growth for the two periods.		
Exponential Trend Coefficient	4.116	3.604	0.504
t-statistic	23.27	10.10	9.47
Chow Test	$S_1 = 2.0495;\ S_2 = 0.3673;\ S_3 = 1.4780;\ S_4 = 1.8453;$ $S_5 = 0.2042;\ F = \frac{(0.2042/2)}{(1.8453/50)} = 2.77$		

contd...

...contd...

	1950-51 to 2003-04	*1950-51 to 1974-75*	*1975-76 to 2003-04*
	The value is less than critical value of $F_{2,50}$ i.e., 3.2, not rejecting the hypothesis of no difference in the growth for the two periods.		
	Area		
Linear Trend Coefficient	0.078	0.058	0.104
t-statistic	14.03	12.10	5.64
Chow Test	$S_1 = 21.0654;\ S_2 = 0.6806;\ S_3 = 18.4540;\ S_4 = 2.5227;$ $S_5 = 18.5427;\ F = \frac{(18.5427/2)}{(2.5227/50)} = 2.52$		
	The value is less than critical value of $F_{2,50}$ i.e., 3.2, not rejecting the hypothesis of no difference in the growth for the two periods.		
Exponential Trend Coefficient	2.000	2.078	2.238
t-statistic	18.23	11.71	6.20
	Yield		
Linear Trend Coefficient	12.740	6.820	19.529
t-statistic	15.45	4.39	9.17
Chow Test	$S_1 = 463583.5;\ S_2 = 72210.1;\ S_3 = 248482.6;\ S_4 = 320692.7;$ $S_5 = 142890.8;\ F = \frac{(142890.8/2)}{(320692.7/50)} = 11.14$		
	The value exceeds critical value of $F_{2,50}$ i.e., 3.2, rejecting the hypothesis of no difference in the growth for the two periods.		
Exponential Trend Coefficient	2.073	1.485	2.745
t-statistic	16.71	4.12	8.86
Chow Test	$S_1 = 1.0282;\ S_2 = 0.3819;\ S_3 = 0.5120;\ S_4 = 0.8939;$ $S_5 = 0.1343;\ F = \frac{(0.1343/2)}{(0.8939/50)} = 3.75$		
	The value exceeds critical value of $F_{2,50}$ i.e., 3.2, rejecting the hypothesis of no difference in the growth for the two periods.		

Cotton

Until recently, cotton was a successful cash crop in India. Area and yield expansion was impressive. Area went up from 6.22 million hectares in 1950/1952 to 7.46 million hectares in 1974/1976 (Table 2.15a). It then went up to 8.14 million hectares in 2001/2003. There was a steady increase in yield from 0.86 quintals per hectare in 1950/1952 to 1.50 quintals per hectare in 1974/1976 and then to 2.29 quintals in 2001-2003. Output goes up from 3.16 million tonnes in 1950/1952 to 6.56 million tonnes in 1974/1976. It was 10.83 million tonnes in 2001/2003.

Table 2.15a

All India Production, Area and Yield of Cotton, Triennium Averages

Area in million hectares; Production in million tonnes; Yield in kgs/hec

	3 YR AVG 1950-1952	3 YR AVG 1974-1976	3 YR AVG 2001/2003
Area	6.22	7.46	8.14
Production	3.16	6.56	10.83
Yield	87	150	229

Output growth goes up from 2.57 per cent annual in the period 1950/1975 to 3.1 per cent annual during 1975/2004 (Table 2.15b). Area growth rate is low, 0.56 per cent annual in the first phase and 0.50 per cent annual in the second. Growth is largely sourced from productivity expansion, with yield leveling off from 2 per cent compound annual in the period 1950/1975 to 1.96 per cent annual in the period 1975/2004.

Table 2.15b

Area, Production and Yield Trends of Cotton 1950/51 to 2003/04

Cotton		Production			Area			Yield		
		1950-51 to 2003-04	1950-51 to 1974-75	1975-76 to 2003-04	1950-51 to 2003-04	1950-51 to 1974-75	1975-76 to 2003-04	1950-51 to 2003-04	1950-51 to 1974-75	1975-76 to 2003-04
Linear	b	0.16	0.12	0.22	0.02	0.04	0.04	3.21	2.25	3.80
	t	15.14	7.47	6.31	3.43	2.66	2.84	14.70	7.22	5.34
Compound	b	2.38	2.57	2.397	0.24	0.56	0.50	2.07	2.00	1.97
	t	18.33	7.29	6.64	3.37	2.76	2.76	18.33	7.49	5.70

Note: Units as in Table 2.15a; b: annual growth rate; t: t-statistic.

Table 2.15c shows that the trend estimates are significantly different between the two periods.

Table 2.15c

Tests of Significance of Growth Rate Differences in the Periods 1950-51 to 1974-75 and 1975-76 to 2003-04

	1950-51 to 2003-04	1950-51 to 1974-75	1975-76 to 2003-04
	Production		
Linear Trend Coefficient	0.164	0.122	0.216
t-statistic	15.14	7.47	6.31

contd...

...contd...

	1950-51 to 2003-04	*1950-51 to 1974-75*	*1975-76 to 2003-04*
Chow Test	$S_1 = 80.5124$; $S_2 = 7.9446$; $S_3 = 64.4801$; $S_4 = 72.4247$; $S_5 = 8.0877$; $F = \frac{(8.0877/2)}{(72.4247/50)} = 2.79$ The value is less than critical value of $F_{2,50}$ i.e., 3.2, not rejecting the hypothesis of no difference in the growth for the two periods.		
Exponential Trend Coefficient	2.322	2.566	2.397
t-statistic	18.33	7.29	6.64
Chow Test	$S_1 = 1.0698$; $S_2 = 0.3614$; $S_3 = 0.6977$; $S_4 = 1.0591$; $S_5 = 0.0107$; $F = \frac{(0.0107/2)}{(1.0591/50)} = 0.25$ The value is less than critical value of $F_{2,50}$ i.e., 3.2, not rejecting the hypothesis of no difference in the growth for the two periods.		
	Area		
Linear Trend Coefficient	0.018	0.039	0.0405
t-statistic	3.43	2.66	2.84
Chow Test	$S_1 = 19.5418$; $S_2 = 6.3534$; $S_3 = 11.1329$; $S_4 = 17.4863$; $S_5 = 2.0555$; $F = \frac{(2.0555/2)}{(17.4863/50)} = 2.94$ The value is less than critical value of $F_{2,50}$ i.e., 3.2, not rejecting the hypothesis of no difference in the growth for the two periods.		
Exponential Trend Coefficient	0.237	0.563	0.498
t-statistic	3.37	2.76	2.76
	Yield		
Linear Trend Coefficient	3.214	2.254	3.803
t-statistic	14.70	7.22	5.34
Chow Test	$S_1 = 32617.62$; $S_2 = 2912.47$; $S_3 = 27802.22$; $S_4 = 30714.69$; $S_5 = 1902.93$; $F = \frac{(1902.93/2)}{(30714.69/50)} = 1.55$ The value is less than critical value of $F_{2,50}$ i.e., 3.2, not rejecting the hypothesis of no difference in the growth for the two periods.		

contd...

...contd...

	1950-51 to 2003-04	*1950-51 to 1974-75*	*1975-76 to 2003-04*
Exponential Trend Coefficient	2.074	1.996	1.974
t-statistic	18.33	7.49	5.70
Chow Test	$S_1 = 0.8558$; $S_2 = 0.2082$; $S_3 = 0.6440$; $S_4 = 0.8522$; $S_5 = 0.0036$; $F = \frac{(0.0036/2)}{(0.8522/50)} = 0.11$ The value is less than critical value of $F_{2,50}$ i.e., 3.2, not rejecting the hypothesis of no difference in the growth for the two periods.		

Jute and Mesta

Jute and mesta is a crop which has shown steady growth in the last century (Table 2.16a). Area went up by roughly 0.3 million hectares in each of the sub-periods. Output more than doubled rising from 4.45 million tonnes in 1950/1952 to 11.39 million tonnes in 2001/2003. Yield went up from 1048 kgs/hec in 1950/1952 to 1135 kgs/hec in 1974/1976 and then rose faster to 1997 kgs/hec in 2001/2003.

Table 2.16a

All India Production, Area and Yield of Jute and Mesta, Triennium Averages

Area in million hectares; Production in million tonnes; Yield in kgs/hec

	3 YR AVG 1950-1952	*3 YR AVG 1974-1976*	*3 YR AVG 2001/2003*
Area	0.76	0.99	1.30
Production	4.45	5.98	11.39
Yield	1048	1135	1997

The growth rate of output remains within the range of 1.9 to 1.7 per cent compound annual in the two sub-periods (Table 2.16b). Area growth of 1.6 per cent compound annual falls to a negative rate of around half of one per cent in the second period, 1975/2004. The yield rate goes up from 0.26 per cent annual in the period 1950/1975 to 2.22 per cent annual in the period 1975/2004.

Table 2.16b

Area, Production and Yield Trends of Jute and Mesta 1950/51 to 2003/04

Jute and Mesta		*Production*			*Area*			*Yield*		
		1950-51 to 2003-04	*1950-51 to 1974-75*	*1975-76 to 2003-04*	*1950-51 to 2003-04*	*1950-51 to 1974-75*	*1975-76 to 2003-04*	*1950-51 to 2003-04*	*1950-51 to 1974-75*	*1975-76 to 2003-04*
Linear	b	0.12	0.10	0.15	0.02	0.01	-0.01	18.84	2.94	33.12
	t	11.47	2.99	5.91	1.30	2.97	-2.00	15.40	1.45	20.10
Compound	b	1.62	1.87	1.70	0.25	1.60	-0.49	1.38	0.26	2.22
	t	10.95	3.11	6.25	1.69	3.17	-1.96	16.11	1.32	18.48

Note: Units as in Table 2.16a; b: annual growth rate; t: t-statistic.

The area and production growth rates are not significantly different from each other in the two periods, but the yield growth rates are. (Table 2.16c).

Table 2.16c

Tests of Significance of Growth Rate Differences in the Periods 1950-51 to 1974-75 and 1975-76 to 2003-04

	1950-51 to 2003-04	*1950-51 to 1974-75*	*1975-76 to 2003-04*
	Production		
Linear Trend Coefficient	0.117	0.100	0.149
t-statistic	11.47	2.99	5.91
Chow Test	$S_1 = 70.5676;\ S_2 = 33.2186;\ S_3 = 34.7046;$ $S_4 = 67.9232;$ $S_5 = 2.6444;\ F = \frac{(2.6444/2)}{(67.9232/50)} = 0.97$ The value is less than critical value of $F_{2,50}$ i.e., 3.2, not rejecting the hypothesis of no difference in the growth for the two periods.		
Exponential Trend Coefficient	1.623	1.872	1.698
t-statistic	10.95	3.11	6.25
Chow Test	$S_1 = 1.4747;\ S_2 = 1.0661;\ S_3 = 0.3974;\ S_4 = 1.4635;$ $S_5 = 0.0112;\ F = \frac{(0.0112/2)}{(1.4635/50)} = 0.19$ The value is less than critical value of $F_{2,50}$ i.e., 3.2, not rejecting the hypothesis of no difference in the growth for the two periods.		

contd...

...contd...

	1950-51 to 2003-04	1950-51 to 1974-75	1975-76 to 2003-04
	Area		
Linear Trend Coefficient	0.018	0.014	-0.006
t-statistic	1.30	2.97	-2.00
Chow Test	$S_1 = 1.4111$; $S_2 = 0.6568$; $S_3 = 0.4489$; $S_4 = 1.1057$; $S_5 = 0.3054$; $F = \frac{(0.3057/2)}{(1.1057/50)} = 6.90$ The value exceeds critical value of $F_{2,50}$ i.e., 3.2, rejecting the hypothesis of no difference in the growth for the two periods.		
Exponential Trend Coefficient	0.247	1.599	-0.491
t-statistic	1.69	3.17	-1.96
	Yield		
Linear Trend Coefficient	18.84	2.936	33.124
t-statistic	15.40	1.45	20.10
Chow Test	$S_1 = 1021785$; $S_2 = 122928.9$; $S_3 = 148893.2$; $S_4 = 271822.1$; $S_5 = 749962.9$; $F = \frac{(749962.9/2)}{(271822.1/50)} = 68.98$ The value exceeds critical value of $F_{2,50}$ i.e., 3.2, rejecting the hypothesis of no difference in the growth for the two periods.		
Exponential Trend Coefficient	1.380	0.263	2.217
t-statistic	16.11	1.32	18.48
Chow Test	$S_1 = 0.4936$; $S_2 = 0.1193$; $S_3 = 0.0771$; $S_4 = 0.1964$; $S_5 = 0.2972$; $F = \frac{(0.2972/2)}{(0.1964/50)} = 37.82$ The value exceeds critical value of $F_{2,50}$ i.e., 3.2, rejecting the hypothesis of no difference in the growth for the two periods.		

Sugarcane

Area expansion in sugarcane has been high. Area under the crop has gone up from 1.83 million hectares in 1950/1952 to 2.83 million hectares in 1974/1976. It further went up to 4.31 million hectares in 2001/2003 (Table 2.17a). Sugarcane is a favourite crop if there is industrial demand for it, since it assures an income to the farmer. Production went up from 59.34 million tones in 1950/1952 to 142.45 million tonnes in 1974/1976 and 277.3 million tonnes in 2001/2003.

Yield correspondingly rose from 32.6 tonnes/hec to 50.4 tonnes in 1974/1976 and then rose to 63.3 tonnes/hec in 2001/2003.

Table 2.17a

All India Production, Area and Yield of Sugarcane, Triennium Averages

Area in million hectares; Production in million tonnes; Yield in kgs/hec

	3 YR AVG 1950-1952	*3 YR AVG 1974-1976*	*3 YR AVG 2001/2003*
Area	1.83	2.83	4.31
Production	59.34	142.45	277.30
Yield	32604	50379	63301

The area expansion growth rate went up from 0.05 per cent compound annual in the period 1950/51-1974/75 to 0.06 per cent compound annual in the period 1975/76-2003/04. Yield growth was negative at minus 2.21 per cent annual in the period 1950/51-1974/75 and 1.07 per cent annual compound in the period 1975/76-2003/04 (Table 2.17b). The output growth rate which was 4.48 per cent compound annual in the first phase went down to 2.84 per cent compound annual in the second phase.

Table 2.17b

Area, Production and Yield Trends of Sugarcane (Cane) 1950/51 to 2003/04

Sugarcane (Cane)		*Production*			*Area*			*Yield*		
		1950-51 to 2003-04	*1950-51 to 1974-75*	*1975-76 to 2003-04*	*1950-51 to 2003-04*	*1950-51 to 1974-75*	*1975-76 to 2003-04*	*1950-51 to 2003-04*	*1950-51 to 1974-75*	*1975-76 to 2003-04*
Linear	b	4.76	3.86	5.96	0.05	0.05	0.06	754.74	879.71	639.04
	t	28.22	11.77	12.71	24.15	7.55	12.15	24.91	11.30	7.51
Compound	b	3.30	4.48	2.84	1.75	2.14	1.75	1.54	2.21	1.07
	t	27.69	11.17	12.60	22.74	7.32	11.81	22.04	11.07	7.51

Note: Units as in Table 2.17a; b: annual growth rate; t: t-statistic.

Table 2.17c shows that area and output growth estimates are significantly different between the two sub-periods and so are the compound yield growth estimates.

Table 2.17c

Tests of Significance of Growth Rate Differences in the Periods 1950-51 to 1974-75 and 1975-76 to 2003-04

	1950-51 to 2003-04	1950-51 to 1974-75	1975-76 to 2003-04
	Production		
Linear Trend Coefficient	4.756	3.875	5.956
t-statistic	28.22	11.77	12.71
Chow Test	$S_1 = 19380.9$; $S_2 = 3238.3$; $S_3 = 12040.6$; $S_4 = 15278.9$; $S_5 = 4102.0$; $F = \frac{(4102.0/2)}{(15278.9/50)} = 6.71$		
	The value exceeds critical value of $F_{2,50}$ i.e., 3.2, rejecting the hypothesis of no difference in the growth for the two periods.		
Exponential Trend Coefficient	3.30	4.477	2.840
t-statistic	27.69	11.17	12.60
Chow Test	$S_1 = 0.9403$; $S_2 = 0.4595$; $S_3 = 0.2709$; $S_4 = 0.7304$; $S_5 = 0.2099$; $F = \frac{(0.2099/2)}{(0.7304/50)} = 7.18$		
	The value exceeds critical value of $F_{2,50}$ i.e., 3.2, rejecting the hypothesis of no difference in the growth for the two periods.		
	Area		
Linear Trend Coefficient	0.049	0.046	0.061
t-statistic	24.15	7.55	12.15
Chow Test	$S_1 = 2.8323$; $S_2 = 1.1109$; $S_3 = 1.3829$; $S_4 = 2.4948$; $S_5 = 0.3375$; $F = \frac{(0.3375/2)}{(2.4948/50)} = 3.38$		
	The value exceeds critical value of $F_{2,50}$ i.e., 3.2, rejecting the hypothesis of no difference in the growth for the two periods.		
Exponential Trend Coefficient	1.75	2.158	1.754
t-statistic	22.74	7.32	11.81
	Yield		
Linear Trend Coefficient	754.74	879.705	639.054
t-statistic	24.91	11.30	7.51

contd...

...contd...

	1950-51 to 2003-04	*1950-51 to 1974-75*	*1975-76 to 2003-04*
Chow Test	$S_1 = 6.26E+08;\ S_2 = 1.81E+08;\ S_3 = 3.97E+08;$ $S_4 = 2.78E+08;$ $S_5 = 4.80E+07;\ F = \frac{(4.80E+07/2)}{(5.78E+08/50)} = 2.08$ The value is less than critical value of $F_{2,50}$ i.e., 3.2, not rejecting the hypothesis of no difference in the growth for the two periods.		
Exponential Trend Coefficient	1.54	2.210	1.065
t-statistic	22.04	11.07	7.51
Chow Test	$S_1 = 0.3263;\ S_2 = 0.1164;\ S_3 = 0.1091;\ S_4 = 0.2255;$ $S_5 = 0.1008;\ F = \frac{(0.1008/2)}{(0.2255/50)} = 11.17$ The value exceeds critical value of $F_{2,50}$ i.e., 3.2, rejecting the hypothesis of no difference in the growth for the two periods.		

Potato

There has been an argument that in the recent period there has been a rapid expansion of vegetable and fruit crops. It is difficult to test on account of data, particularly in a long historical sweep. Potatoes are a crop for which reasonably robust data is available for the period of our analysis. Since the horticultural argument is largely demand-based, analysis of a crop should be helpful. The output of potatoes has indeed grown rapidly in the period from 1974/1976-2001-2003. It has gone up from 6.77 million tonnes to 23.59 million tonnes. In the earlier period, it also went up from 1.69 million tonnes to 6.77 million tonnes. (Table 2.18a).

The growth rate of output was high at 4.87 per cent compound annual in the period 1975/2004 (Table 2.18b). It was higher at 5.8 per cent annual in the period 1950/1975 but that was from a very low base. Yield growth was 1.61 and 1.67 per cent respectively in the two periods and area growth 3.81 and 2.81 per cent annual.

Table 2.18a

All India Production, Area and Yield of Potato, Triennium Averages

Area in million hectares; Production in million tonnes; Yield in kgs/hec

	3 YR AVG 1950-1952	3 YR AVG 1974-1976	3 YR AVG 2001-2003
Area	0.25	0.61	1.28
Production	1.69	6.77	23.59
Yield	6882.50	11168.00	18553.00

Table 2.18b

Area, Production and Yield Trends of Potato 1950/51 to 2003/04

Potato		Production			Area			Yield		
		1950-51 to 2003-04	1950-51 to 1974-75	1975-76 to 2003-04	1950-51 to 2003-04	1950-51 to 1974-75	1975-76 to 2003-04	1950-51 to 2003-04	1950-51 to 1974-75	1975-76 to 2003-04
Linear	b	0.453	0.168	0.647	0.021	0.014	0.026	260.366	129.391	11607.62
	t	23.67	14.19	19.02	38.81	24.65	22.07	25.36	5.80	28.48
Compound	b	5.74	5.534	4.541	3.34	3.812	2.813	2.31	1.614	1.674
	t	49.60	16.97	21.88	55.26	22.38	23.65	25.17	5.62	10.68

Note: Units as in Table 2.18a; b: annual growth rate; t: t-statistic.

Table 2.18c shows that growth rates are significantly different in the two periods.

Table 2.18c

Tests of Significance of Growth Rate Differences in the Periods 1950-51 to 1974-75 and 1975-76 to 2003-04

	1950-51 to 2003-04	1950-51 to 1974-75	1975-76 to 2003-04
	Production		
Linear Trend Coefficient	0.453	0.168	0.647
t-statistic	23.67	14.19	19.02
Chow Test	$S_1 = 249.757$; $S_2 = 4.194$; $S_3 = 63.464$; $S_4 = 67.658$; $S_5 = 182.099$; $F = \frac{(182.099/2)}{(67.658/50)} = 67.29$		
	The value exceeds critical value of $F_{2,50}$ i.e., 3.2, rejecting the hypothesis of no difference in the growth for the two periods.		
Exponential Trend Coefficient	5.74	5.534	4.541
t-statistic	49.60	16.97	21.88

contd...

...contd...

	1950-51 to 2003-04	*1950-51 to 1974-75*	*1975-76 to 2003-04*
Chow Test	$S_1 = 0.8640;\ S_2 = 0.3013;\ S_3 = 0.2258;\ S_4 = 0.5271;$ $S_5 = 0.3369;\ F = \frac{(0.3369/2)}{(0.5271/50)} = 15.97$ The value exceeds critical value of $F_{2,50}$ i.e., 3.2, rejecting the hypothesis of no difference in the growth for the two periods.		
	Area		
Linear Trend Coefficient	0.021	0.014	0.026
t-statistic	38.81	24.65	22.07
Chow Test	$S_1 = 0.2054;\ S_2 = 0.0100;\ S_3 = 0.0782;\ S_4 = 0.0882;$ $S_5 = 0.1172;\ F = \frac{(0.1172/2)}{(0.0882/50)} = 33.24$ The value exceeds critical value of $F_{2,50}$ i.e., 3.2, rejecting the hypothesis of no difference in the growth for the two periods.		
Exponential Trend Coefficient	3.34	3.812	2.813
t-statistic	55.26	22.38	23.65
	Yield		
Linear Trend Coefficient	260.366	129.391	11607.62
t-statistic	25.36	5.80	28.48
Chow Test	$S_1 = 71919211;\ S_2 = 14885558;\ S_3 = 30873075;$ $S_4 = 45758633;$ $S_5 = 26160578;\ F = \frac{(26160578/2)}{(45758633/50)} = 14.29$ The value exceeds critical value of $F_{2,50}$ i.e., 3.2, rejecting the hypothesis of no difference in the growth for the two periods.		
Exponential Trend Coefficient	2.31	1.614	1.674
t-statistic	25.17	5.62	10.68
Chow Test	$S_1 = 0.5616;\ S_2 = 0.2422;\ S_3 = 0.1326;\ S_4 = 0.3748;$ $S_5 = 0.1868;\ F = \frac{(0.1868/2)}{(0.3748/50)} = 12.46$ The value exceeds critical value of $F_{2,50}$ i.e., 3.2, rejecting the hypothesis of no difference in the growth for the two periods.		

Conclusions

The agricultural sector is traditionally regarded as having low price responses. Also, as regards crop choices it is the agro-climatic regimes which determine possibilities. In India on top of the basic factors, the sector was also subject to State policies, in terms of price and quantity interventions in markets. India is a big country so there are differences in resource endowments which designate the agro-climatic environment. Cropping patterns will be different in different areas, also because these factors are of a long-term or permanent nature and there is a kind of basic stability in cropping patterns. They do change because of economic reasons or technological reasons but the change is slower. Another factor is that from the decade of the fifties of the last century onwards there have been great changes particularly from the sixties in technology, namely the seed fertiliser technology. But the technologies adopted are in different areas with different seeds and this is also true of different crops. So again there are different cropping patterns and different rates of agricultural growth cropping patterns depend on technological factors, economic factors and institutional factors.

The economic factors are maximisation of expected returns and economic returns will depend on prices of output and inputs. Inspite of the factors outlined, market reform would also impact. The extent of control was not the same for all commodities. Also, there were changes in policies.

Regarding food grains, there is remarkable underlying stability in area and a rapid increase in yield. The latter is particularly so from the mid-sixties. Since the mid-seventies yield almost doubles. Area is constant in the period 1966/1968 to 2003/2004, declining in the *kharif* and rising in the *rabi*. *Rabi* shares of production have been rising.

Yield increase of food grains per year was almost three times more in 1975-76 to 2003/04 at 31.31 kg/ha per year as compared to 12.46 kg/ha per year in 1950-51 to 1974-75. Thus, yield expansion which was around 13 kgs per hectare in the first period rose to around 32 kgs per hectare in the second period.

In the second period, we see the interesting phenomenon of a much higher quantum of grains being produced with some land being actually released for other non-food grain crops. This takes place on account of a rapid increase in yield. Indian agriculture comes of age with diversification of the cropping base in relation presumably to demand arising from faster economic growth within the context of limited land reserves.

In rice, area growth continues in the second period. Output almost doubles in the second phase largely from productivity growth. Wheat was the crop in which the Green Revolution began. Area doubles in the first phase. Area growth in the second phase was lower. It was higher in rice in that phase. Rice was the crop of the second phase. Output goes up by four times in the first phase and then growth is less. Production increased in the second period faster, area increased twice more in the first period. Yield obviously increased faster in the second period. Wheat is definitely the crop of the late sixties and seventies, just as rice is of the second period i.e.,1975-76/2003-04.

There has been through the half century a movement away from coarse cereals. However, it is also true that coarse cereals were a dry land crop and productivity in the dry land areas did not keep pace, both on account of infrastructural bottlenecks and technological neglect. Maize is a crop in which there has been output and productivity growth through the period. Maize is not only consumed as a staple but is also important as poultry feed and as an input for the starch industry and use for these non-food/agricultural activities has been expanding. Yield went up from around 5 quintals per hectare to around a tonne in the period 1950/51 to 1975/76. It further grew from 1.08 tonnes/hec in 1975/76 to 1.79 tonnes/hec by 2003/04. Area expansion was negligible in the second period in which output almost doubled from 6.41 million tonnes to 11.31 million tonnes.

Area under pulses rises from around 19 million hectares to 23 lakh hectares in the first phase and then stagnates. The output expansion in the second phase, significantly higher than the first phase, is sourced from yield.

Oilseeds are important crops of the Indian agricultural economy. They are in fact prominent in the rainfed and dry land areas and for a long period irrigated area under oilseeds was marginal and is still low. Area under oilseeds has expanded, in some areas at the expense of grain crops, for example, sunflower or mustard in *rabi* in north India and groundnut in Gujarat, Maharashtra and Andhra Pradesh, in others by cropping on earlier fallows, for example, soya farming in *kharif* fallows in Madhya Pradesh and in yet others with increase in cropping intensity with irrigation, particularly in areas where water deltas are low. Area under oilseeds goes up by around 35 to 50 per cent in the two phases.

We contrast groundnut with mustard. Area under groundnut increases from 4.71 million hectares in 1950/1952 to 7.14 million hectares in 1974/1976. It then falls to 6.06 million hectares until 2001/2003. (Table 2.13a). Groundnut production increases from 3.34 million tonnes in 1950/1952 to 5.94 million tonnes in 1974/1976 and is placed at 6.44 million tonnes in 2001/2003. In groundnut, output growth rate declines in the second period from 2.01 per cent compound annual in the period 1950/51-1975/76 to 0.69 per cent annual in the period 1975/1976-2001/2003. Rapeseed and mustard is the rising crop in the oilseed sector. Output grows up from 0.85 million tonnes in 1950/1952 to 2.1 million tonnes in 1974/1976 and further to 4.99 million tonnes in 2001/2003. Area goes up from 2.24 million hectares in 1950/1952 to 3.51 million hectares in 1974/1976 and then more than doubles at 5 million hectares in 2001/2003. Yield rises from 3.8 quintals in 1950/1952 to 5.96 quintals in 1974/1976 and then a much higher increase to over a tonne (10.31 quintals).

In term of growth rates there is a near doubling factor in yield and output determining the growth trajectory. Area growth increases from 2.08 per cent compound annual in the first phase to 2.24 per cent annual in the second phase and yield growth increases from 1.49 per cent compound annual to 2.75 per cent compound annual. Output growth, therefore, increases from 3.6 per cent compound annual in the period 1950/51-1975/76 to 5.04 per cent compound annual in 1975/76 to 2001-2003.

Until recently cotton was a successful cash crop in India. Area and yield expansion was impressive. Area went up from 6.22 million hectares in 1950/1952 to 7.46 million hectares in 1974/1976 and to 8.14 million hectares in 2001/2003. Output goes up from 3.16 million tonnes in 1950/1952 to 6.56 million tonnes in 1974/1976. It was 10.83 million tonnes in 2001/2003.

Output growth goes up from 2.57 per cent annual in the period 1950/1975 to 3.1 per cent annual during 1976/2003. Area growth rate is low; 0.56 per cent annual in the first phase and 0.50 per cent annual in the second. Growth is largely sourced from productivity expansion, with yield leveling off from 2 per cent compound annual in the period 1950/ 1975 to 1.96 per cent annual in the period 1975/2003.

Jute and mesta is a crop which has shown steady growth in the last century. Area went up by roughly 0.3 million hectares in each of the sub-periods. Output more than doubled rising from 4.45 million tonnes in 1950/1952 to 11.39 million tonnes in 2001/2003.

Sugarcane is a favourite crop if there is industrial demand for it, since it assures an income to the farmer. Area expansion in sugarcane has been high. Area under the crop has gone up from 1.83 million hectares in 1950/1952 to 2.83 million hectares in 1974/1976. It further went up to 4.31 million hectares in 2001/2003. Yield rose from 32.6 tonnes/hec to 50.4 tonnes in 1974/1976 and then rose to 63.3 tonnes/ hec in 2001/2003.

There has been an argument that in the recent period there has been a rapid expansion of vegetable and fruit crops. The output of potatoes has indeed grown rapidly in the period from 1974/1976-2003/ 2004. It has gone up from 6.77 million tonnes to 24.31 million tonnes. The growth rate of output was high at 4.87 per cent compound annual in the period 1975/2004. It was higher at 5.8 per cent annual in the period 1950/1975, but that was from a very low base.

At a more general level, while there have been a number of studies of growth in Indian agriculture as noted at the outset in this chapter, they have been of a descriptive type. Also the periodisation has either been decades or the availability of data as in the classic studies by Prof. Bhalla and his associates (Bhalla and Alagh, 1979; Bhalla and Singh, 2002). Our interest is in unraveling underlying trends which would give us an insight to model behaviour of the agricultural economy. Our interest is in demand and supply factors underlying crop level performance. The analysis by periods of slower and faster economy level growth is important.

We have conducted Chow tests for a number of crops above to see if the estimates of trend growth in production, area and productivity are different between the two periods 1950/1975 and 1975/2004. Out of the 72 tests we have conducted, in 54 tests the differences in the trend estimates are statistically significant. There is, therefore, overwhelming evidence to suggest that in many crops, the two periods reflect structurally different growth paradigms.

This preliminary exercise is to set, as it were the background for this analysis. This would then give us insights as to whether the Indian agricultural economy would respond to market dominated signals. The significantly different supply features in the two periods, 1950/1975 and 1975/2004, suggest differential responses to economic stimuli in the period of slower growth of the economy and the faster growth period. Also, they suggest that parts of the agrarian economy may respond in different ways to market signals. These are, however testable hypotheses and if we move towards better understanding of underlying behaviour, better policies may eventually follow. Better understanding by itself is important for a modest research effort.

3 Aggregate Agricultural Supply Function of India

Introduction

This chapter works on the problem of an aggregate agricultural supply function for India. The problem was posed in the first chapter where the argument of supply responding to prices was posed in the context of influential mega studies of the Indian agricultural economy with the work of scholars like Prof. Dantwala, Prof. Hanumantha Rao, Dr. Tyagi and others. We now begin with a review of the technical literature. There is a degree of repetition but now the emphasis is on models and empirical studies. We begin with the theoretical literature on aggregate supply analysis, particularly the question on lags in response to price stimuli in the agricultural sector emerging from the time period characteristics of crop production. Given the seasonal nature of agricultural production, supply comes with a lag, depending on the crop calendar. This characteristic of the agricultural economy is recognised at the textbook level and we summarise the main outlines of the received theory and recent developments.

We then review the Indian studies on the subject, laying out the arguments of the elasticity pessimists and optimists. We begin with the arguments presented by influential Indian economists that while allocation to resources at the crop level can be price elastic, this need not be so at the level of the agricultural sector as a whole. (Chakravarty, 1974; Bapna, 1980 and many others). The sometimes mildly different, at other times contrary arguments are also presented, by scholars like Raj Krishna (1967), Kahlon and Tyagi (1983) and more recently Hazell and Mishra (1996) and many others.

We then present an alternate strand of reasoning to the effect that both the arguments may have relevance at particular phases of the development of the economy and within the context of the stage of macro reform the economy is at. This stand is triggered by our analysis of trends in the Indian economy, which concludes, to recapitulate briefly for completeness:

> The significantly different supply features in the two periods, 1950/1975 and 1975/2004, suggest differential responses to economic stimuli in the period of slower growth of the economy and the faster growth period. Also, they suggest that parts of the agrarian economy may respond in different ways to market signals. These are however, testable hypotheses and if we move towards better understanding of underlying behaviour, better policies may eventually follow.

This kind of approach emerges also from the fact that while it has been the tradition to label economists and scholars as elasticity pessimists and optimists, not necessarily in these words but in sense, in fact the greats of Indian economics were eclectic scholars, borrowing from each other and stating differences in a nuanced manner. Interestingly, S. Chakravarty, while labelled as an agricultural surplus theorist, was against the position of treating agriculture as a "bargain sector" and Raj Krishna was very clear that price responsiveness cannot be expected if transport and market infrastructure do not exist. Both of them also showed an acute awareness of the sensitivity of empirical estimates to policy stimuli. Time phasing and sectoral disaggregation would also emerge from growth patterns of the economy and the larger policy context in which the agricultural sector participates.

We specify alternate models which are time phase and policy system specific. These are empirically tested. It is shown that price responsiveness is there only for the periods and the sections of the agricultural economy in which market features predominate. In the final section it is argued that policy to agriculture is very muddled at the present stage working with a folklore which is not fully relevant. We also show the scope for further work.

The Theoretical Frame

Acreage Response

Many significant studies have been done with regard to acreage response in India. Acreage response means changes in price being correlated not with changes in quantity but with changes in acreage.

Acreage is a measure of the crop the farmer intended to produce, hence acreage can quite legitimately be used as a proxy for output. However, the procedure has some limitations. As acreage is taken as a proxy variable, there is a built-in tendency for under-calculating supply elasticity when a major crop has a dominant share in the menu of crops. Another major limitation of acreage response in its very nature is that it does not take cognizance of the farmers need or actual attempts to intensify his production by changes in the intensity of land use and through the use of fertilisers and technology.

The elasticity of output is the summation of the elasticities of acreage and the summation of the elasticity of yield per acre. Thus, acreage elasticity underestimates the real price elasticity. This is especially true for major crops and other crops where production can be increased by applying larger quantities of inputs. Another significant condition for underestimation of yield is a situation where yield responds to exogenous variables such as price, irrigation and technology. So the elasticity of planned production will differ from the elasticity of planted area. Clearly acreage elasticity is synonymous or approximates output elasticity only under static agriculture assumptions.

Raj Krishna argued that the price elasticities of acreage are considered to be good minimum approximations of the elasticities of output on the assumption that when the acreage in a crop is varied, other inputs can be varied *pari passu*, and over the relevant ranges of the production functions, returns to scale are not diminishing. (Krishna, 1967: 504). Subsistence crops are seen by him to fall into the low response range whereas commercial crops in the high response range.

Supply: The Time Element

Supply is also not always quick in response to price. In fact increase in production to a given increase in price varies with the time allowed for adjustments to take place. If a longer time is allowed for adjustment to take place, the quantity supplied is more responsive to a given price change. Clearly as time goes on from the very short-run (when supply is a vertical line) to the long-run (when supply curves became flatter) when more time is given prior to harvest, more number of variables and more among of particular variables can be changed whereas in the short-run, the amongst of inputs such as fertilisers applied to crops can be varied in the longer run and the area planted under crops can be changed. The short-run period varies among commodities and this time dimension is different for different commodities. In the short-run period some factors are variable and in the long-run period we consider all factors to be variable. Clearly in the long-run period there is no fixed factor: the acreage can be increased, buildings can be altered, additional labour and new machinery can be acquired.

It is textbook understanding that farming is incapable of reacting immediately to changes in price (Hill and Ray, 1987: Ch.10) by altering the level of output. The response of farmers is thought to consist of two stages, each with its separate time lag. The first is the expectations time lag, and describes the time it takes for farmers to recognise a price change and to be convinced that it is sufficiently permanent to be worth responding to. The second relates to the delay in adjusting to the now perceived and assessed price shift. Strictly what we are measuring when relating output changes to price movements is an estimate of actual response rather than of the amounts that farmers wish to supply under the new price relations. Nevertheless, it is the actual response which is of importance as far as governments are concerned when they are trying to manipulate agricultural markets with policy intentions in mind. Clearly, higher prices are associated with greater output. The long-term coefficients are larger than the short-term ones.

Supply analysis theoreticians have also pointed out that prices themselves may change in structure through time. Thus, Askari and Cummings state:

> the most appropriate price variable of ten years ago may no longer be relevant today. For example, if farmers become more prosperous and educated, they may well buy a much wider range of consumer products. Though we would contend that in the early stages of development the consumer price index would not be an appropriate deflator, when might it become so? (Askari and Cummings, 1977: 259)

Cost Structure and Supply Elasticity

Another factor determining the rate at which farmers respond to price changes is the cost structure of production. The distinction made here has to be between variable and fixed costs of production. However, it should be pointed out that the distinction is not absolute and will depend on the time span under consideration. While within a short period, say a month, the rent which a farmer has to pay, the interest he faces on a mortgage and his wage bill for regular labour, would be considered as fixed cost, the longer the time period in which costs are viewed, the more that becomes variable. The farm labour force can be adjusted, the size of farm changed and so on.

The implication of cost structure, in the form of the balance between fixed and variable costs, applies to the greatest extent in the response to falling prices. The higher the proportion of fixed costs, the smaller will be the tendency to cut output when output prices fall, that is, supply will be less elastic. As an industry, agriculture seems to have a comparatively large proportion of its total costs in a fixed form.

Within the labour force in agriculture the family accounts for an increasing proportion of the total cost as hired labour is shed. Again this represents a rise in the share of costs which are fixed, in that it is easier to displace hired workers on a family farm in response to falling farm profits coming from lower prices than to shed family members. Consequently there will be a tendency to continue production and absorb falling profitability by taking a smaller income and tightening the proverbial belt. In supply terms, this means a lower elasticity.

These kinds of issues were not supposed to have relevance to Indian agriculture but the share of family labour is high, although the trend is towards more casualisation of the labour force. In a market economy of the kind, economic policy in India is pushing and relative profitability gives signals for resource allocation. The earlier arguments, that as long as land productivity is rising, there is no cause of worry are no longer valid. In a market economy, profitability gives powerful signals for resource allocation, both for the short-run and equally important for investment. Profitability of resource use is important, not just productivity of land. We have to move over from a Ricardian to a Haberler point of view at the micro level. Not just land productivity but profitability of resource use gives signals at the margin for resource use.

Agricultural profitability in India falls by 14.2 per cent through the decade of economic reforms, as the following estimates show and this would have economic consequences as discussed above.

Table 3.1

Agricultural Prices Paid and Received

S.No.	Period	Prices Paid for Intermediates	Output Prices
1	1990/91	104.0	112.3
2	2000/01	223.0	224.8
3	% change 1990/91–2000/01	114.4	100.2

Source: Computed from estimates given in CACP, 2003, Table 5.1, p.297.

Transfer Earnings of Factors and Supply Elasticity

There is also the question of the opportunities for alternative uses of resources currently engaged on farms when product prices fall, in other words their transfer earnings. Because their transfer earnings are low, farmers especially those found on smaller farms, will tend to stay as producers when prices and incomes decline, giving agricultural production a low supply elasticity. When the general economy is at a low level of development or in a depressed state, with few suitable jobs available outside agriculture, the lack of movement will be even more marked.

With capital assets, a similar picture emerges; here the problem is described as asset fixity. Once acquired and installed on farms, much of the buildings and equipments used by farmers has low resale or scrap values. The same will apply to much farm machinery; lorries and vans may command a price for use in other industries but if a farmer tries to sell his tractor or thresher because of declining cereal prices, he is quite likely to find that the market in second-hand tractors or threshers is depressed because many other farmers are also trying to sell. If the realisable value of an asset is very low, irrespective of what it cost to acquire and install, then the preferable option will often be to continue in production assuming that product prices cover average variable costs.

D. Gale Johnson further develops the theory for the output behavior of agriculture in prosperity and depression. For depression or periods of farm price declines, Johnson finds that the sustained output of agriculture is related to the fact that prices of many inputs based on alternative opportunity costs fall to very low levels. Investments in capital assets and land are sunk costs. Even though product prices are low, the farmer has no alternative use for these assets other than in farm production. It takes time for equipment to wear out and become obsolete. The supply of labour on the family farm is not easily reduced. The maintenance of "other" input schedules works against a reduction in total output. In periods of prosperity agricultural output is more responsive to increases in farm price returns. Agricultural output expands as a result of technological development and increased capital expenditures. Johnson shows that some resources shift in and out of agriculture rather easily and rapidly in response to price, although other resources in the same time period hardly shift at all. (Johnson, 1949: 539-64).

The Indian Background and Analytical Frame

In a seminal article, "Agricultural Price Policy and Economic Development," Raj Krishna writes that the context of agricultural development differs in different parts of the world. It may differ with respect to the demand outlook confronting the agriculture of a country, or the product pattern characterising it, or the resource potential available to it (Krishna, 1967: 497). He discusses excess demand countries and densely settled countries. With regard to agricultural price policy, a historical framework is described; agricultural price policy has generally been used negatively to keep bread and raw materials cheap for the growing industrial sector, and to maximise and transfer to the city for investment of the profits of trade in agricultural commodities.

In other words, the terms of trade of agriculture are deliberately depressed. In this connection he talks of three possible ways in which this may happen. Taxation and price policy have to be considered together. Taxation (or confiscation) of a part of agricultural output can be regarded as the payment of a zero price for that part. The part that is paid for maybe priced low and so act over and above the tax, or even if the price is steady the terms of trade may turn against agriculture if the taxes on agriculture are increased. Thirdly, the prices of urban goods may be raised as opposed to agricultural commodities. Raj Krishna describes the reasons why in many countries, passing through early stages of development, a negative price policy cannot be followed without risking failure to achieve sustained growth. These include reasons like population pressure.

The price responsiveness of Indian agriculture as a whole or the aggregate supply response question is a controversial issue and the protagonists discuss it as an either/or proposition. Raj Krishna has defended positive responsiveness of total production to price and other economic incentives. The empirical studies conducted by Raj Krishna with respect to supply behaviour of agricultural produce use the multiple regression method. Raj Krishna asserts that if the non-price variables are correctly specified, it is possible to obtain significant net regression coefficients and elasticities of price. It cannot be outrightly believed that in less developed countries, output is irresponsive to price changes nor can any general verdict be passed in this respect. However, the responsiveness of output to price varies between crops and regions.

It is generally agreed that at the level of an individual crop, supply is price responsive. The debate arises at the aggregate level. A moment's reflection will show that in transitional policy regime, price responsiveness should be expected to work only for that segment of the agricultural economy where prices have been given a role to play. For example, if there is a sector of the agricultural economy where prices are set by the State, a political process sets a linear rising trend for them, quantities are purchased by the State at those prices, then the farmer will respond to the expectation of linear growth in prices. This will have nothing to do with market prices for the agricultural sector as a whole. But market processes may be at work in the rest of the agricultural economy. Here the distinction is not between crops and the sector but between the market and non-market part of the economy.

Policy economists have argued somewhat powerfully that Indian macro policy is in a transitional phase. In this phase you have price reform in some sectors and others are a part of the transitional regime. In India, the mid-eighties saw the first transition from a regime with output, investment, technology and import control at the commodity level to a regime which would use fiscal and not quantitative controls. In 1985, India designed an extensive programme of reform emphasising internal competition initially. In the mid-eighties, around two-thirds of organised Indian industry was removed from price and quantitative controls to tax and tariff rate interventions. From firm level controls, the economy moved to industry level interventions with strong schemes of incentives and disincentives. These would discriminate between industries but not between firms. It is here that the Indians developed an alternate pattern. The policy framework was seen as a transitional regime, leading later in the early nineties to uniform and low tariff rates and freely convertible exchange rates. However, in many sectors and particularly in the food grains sector, a largely administered regime continued. These nuances need to be modelled in the supply response debates. There would be market and policy dominated segments of the macro economy relating to the agricultural sector. They would follow separate economic laws and this would need to be specified. An attempt is made to do this in this work.

At a conceptual level for the market determined sector, we review the theoretical underpinnings of supply functions, beginning with the Nerlovian framework used in Indian studies. We suggest that at the macro level in which aggregate supply function analysis is conducted, a useful theoretical system may be of a kind in which the decisions of the farm sector as a whole are made in a sequential framework. In the first or primal stage, the farming sector decides to allocate resources to production and economic use in response to economic or relative price stimuli. This decision, mainly committing land or aggregate resources to production would be made in a Nerlovian structure in the phase and for those aspects of the economy of agriculture where price stimuli are allowed to function, in which market structure has developed and price responses matter. Once this decision is made at a sequential level, decisions regarding technology applications would be taken. In an analytical sense, this kind of theoretical system would belong to the class of causal chain systems in empirical work associated with the work of Herman Wold (1953). Policy models have also used causal chain structures as developed by scholars like Chakravarti (1969) and Sengupta and Tintner (1963). The logic of these causal chain systems is briefly described in the next chapter (Chapter 4: 24-25).

This chapter develops a causal chain structure where the decision to commit land resources to production is made in a Nerlovian framework for the market dominated sub-system in the agricultural sector. Once the decision is made, the available technology is committed to production. The technology relation is of a Solow type as applied to the agricultural sector in the well known study by Z. Girliches (1959, 1960). This model is specified and then estimated for the Indian economy for the period 1950/51 to 1996/97 and for the two periods 1950/51 to 1979/80 and 1980/81 to 1996/97. The model does not work for the entire period and for the first period substantiating the stand of the great price response pessimists of Indian agriculture. But the question we attempt to address is if it works for the second phase. Also, in which components of the agricultural macro economy does this system work?

It is obvious that if acreage in the current year depends on prices received in the last year, regressions of this year's prices on acreage will give incorrect results with serial correlation in the error terms. To quote a standard text's discussion of autocorrelation, in a 'cobweb phenomenon': if the farmers overproduce in year t, they are likely to reduce their production in t+1, and so on, leading to a Cobweb pattern (Gujarati, 1995: 404). In this particular case as Klein and Wold have shown, OLS regressions will work as the following section shows.

Causal Chain Systems

These kind of systems are also associated with causal chain analysis as pioneered by Herman Wold (Gureen, 1953). The two crucial features of a recursive system are a triangular B matrix and a diagonal Σ matrix. As an illustration, consider the model

$$y_{1t} + d_{11}X_t = u_{1t}$$

$$b_{21}y_{1t} + y_{2t} + d_{21}X_t = u_{2t}$$

with the specification

$$E(uu') = \Sigma = \begin{bmatrix} \sigma_{11} & 0 \\ 0 & \sigma_{22} \end{bmatrix}$$

To explore the connection between the y's and the u's, we look at the reduced-form equations which are

$y_{1t}=-d_{11}x_t+u_t$

$y_{2t}= (b_{21}d_{11}-d_{21})x_t+(u_{2t}-b_{21}u_{1t})$

The first equation is the same in each case. Since the exogenous variable x is by assumption uncorrelated with the u's, the first equation may be estimated consistently by OLS. The second reduced-form equation shows y_{2t} to be a function of both u_{1t} and u_{2t} Thus, it would be inappropriate to estimate the second structural equation by an OLS regression of y, on y_2 and x. However, y_{1t} is uncorrelated with u_{2t}, since it is a function only of u_{1t} which has zero correlation with u_{2t}. Thus, an OLS regression of y_2 on y_1 and x will yield consistent estimates of the second structural equation.

In the usual analysis, current prices are related to current production. But both price and production may be measured as deviations from their respective time trends. 'Lagged output' now will show how current output is related to past prices. Specifically, output here is lagged one period after price. If output in the first period is q_1, then price is p_1. This leads to an output of q_2 and a price p_2 in the second period and so on.

Any model is recursive if it shows how certain initial conditions will affect conditions in a coming period say t_{+1}, then how conditions in period t_{+2} and so on. The Cobweb model is the simplest recursive model in economics but it is not the only recursive model.[1]

To re-emphasise, "the first equation may be estimated consistently by OLS." And again, "thus an OLS regression of y_2 on y_1 and x will yield

1. The derivation of the cobweb model is described well in a number of textbooks and articles (See Christ, 1966, Section 2-7 page 23-46 and Klien, 1962: Chapters 2 and 5). In this connection, Marc Nerlove's (1956) piece is the classic paper, also his later paper (Nerlove, 1969) which covers basically the concept of how past prices can be used to represent expected prices and how farmers' expectations of future relative prices plays a specific role in shaping their decisions as to how many acres to devote to each crop. The model is well covered in a section on cyclic variations in individual agricultural prices by Geoff Shepherd (1968), which covers the concept of runs. A.S. Goldberger (1964) also specifies the quantitative relations of lags well.

consistent estimates of the second structural equation." (Johnston, 1984: 468).

The Indian Debate

In the late sixties and seventies the dominant sense amongst influential Indian economists was that the aggregate agricultural supply function of the Indian economy was price inelastic. We summarise this from S. Chakravarti, although the argument was present in Dharam Narain (1965), Blynn (1966) and Mitra (1977), amongst others. Chakravarti states, using R. Thamarajakshi's work "that income terms of trade have behaved against the industrial sector." (Chakravarti, 1974: 217). Noting that "the product wage rate has gone up relatively with corresponding decline in the profit margin of the non-agricultural sector" and that the savings rate would be adversely affected, Chakravarti identifies "the inelasticity of the marketed surplus of agriculture as the single most important barrier to growth." (Ibid.: 222).

S.L. Bapna's (1980) empirical validation of the supply inelasticity hypothesis is the most widely cited work. He studied supply response in the agricultural sector in Ajmer district. He tests the following hypothesis:

1) The aggregate supply elasticity of total agricultural production in Ajmer district is positive and low;
2) Aggregate supply elasticity in traditional agriculture (i.e., between the years 1956-57 and 1965-66) is less than in an agriculture in transition from traditional to modern (i.e., between 1966-67 and 1976-77); and
3) Elasticity of supply of both aggregate area and yield is positive but the supply elasticity of area is more than the elasticity of yield.

For the first hypothesis, the elasticity coefficient was found to be 0.24 and was statistically significant at 5 per cent. Interestingly, Bapna in his study assuming different lag structure and weights, classified expected price into two groups on the basis of their means and coefficient of variations. In one exercise he finds, "the estimates of supply elasticities from the second group of prices were unusually high, sometimes exceeding 0.60. Theoretically, such high supply elasticities at the aggregate level are not plausible." (Bapna, 1980: 94). Bapna, therefore, gets a result of elastic aggregate supply but rejects it on a theoretical ground. For the second hypothesis, the conclusion was that although the observed supply elasticity for technologically changing agriculture was more than the elasticity for traditional agriculture, the difference between the two was not much. For the third hypothesis, Bapna concluded that, "supply elasticities for the aggregate area and yield are positive, but for area the elasticity is insignificant and for yield it is significant. This leads us to reject the hypothesis originally proposed" (Ibid., p.105).

Raj Krishna presented the most influential counterfactual. He recognised the role of non-price variables and yet emphasised the importance of price incentives. He argued:

> In measuring the contribution of price movements to agricultural growth we must not lose sight of the fundamental truth that the transformation of traditional agriculture is primarily a techno-organisational episode. The transformation cannot be brought about only or mainly by price movements. However, the techno-organisational effort can be retarded or accelerated by price movements. Favourable price movements can speed up the diffusion of innovations, the absorption of new inputs, the utilisation of idle capacity, and even institutional adjustments. Unfavourable movements can slow down or arrest all these processes. (p.517).

Raj Krishna makes it clear that in an open economy, development of transport, communication, monetisation and commercialisation, will determine the price responsiveness of total output or the lack of it.

> To say that the agriculture of an isolated area is not price responsive is to say something trivially obvious...There is no point in asserting that in all these regions output will or will not be price responsive. And the degree of responsiveness should be expected to differ from region to region. (p.513).

He also makes the point that mono-crop and land surplus export economies will show price responsiveness, if the dominant crop responds to prices and the rest does not fall and surplus land and labour are used for exportable output. Even in densely settled multi-crop agriculture when

> land is reallocated between crops, aggregate output at current prices can be rising even when aggregate physical output (in some sense) is not. (p.515).

Raj Krishna, therefore, establishes the role of price incentives in inducing aggregate production responses. Raj Krishna begins by saying that the context of agricultural development differs in different parts of the world. It may differ with respect to demand outlook confronting the agriculture of a country, or the product pattern characterising it, or the resource potential available to it. Many countries in Western Europe and America face problems created by deceleration of demand and the consequent accumulation of surpluses. Others face a yawning gap between the growth of demand and the available supply. In some countries, agriculture has a fairly diversified product mix but in many others a single crop dominates the mix, occupying 50 to 90 per cent of the total area cultivated. In African and Latin American countries, large tracts of land are still available for settlement and cultivation; but in many Asian countries there is little scope for further land settlement (Krishna, 1967).

India has been experimenting with a slow and step-wise economic reform process. The late eighties and early nineties saw industry and sector level reform. This meant that firm or household level intervention of a quantitative nature were removed and yet there could be differences between sectors, and within a sector, both in the economic incentives designed and the level of intervention by the State. A part of a sector would be under a market and the rest under an administered policy regime.

The interesting point was that this kind of policy regime got considerable attention in the policy debates of the early nineties at the global level. By this time the Bretton woods structural reform was being analysed and alternatives models of globalisation were being discussed. The Indian example was seen as a counterfactual. Lance Taylor in a fairly widely quoted paper described an MPS (Multifaceted Price System) as a "transition from an administered towards a market regime". (Taylor, 1992: 7.) He gave the Polish and Indian examples of "its homely virtues are perhaps becoming more evident". (Ibid. p.7). And the Indians for transitional regimes "developing effective multi-tiered pricing systems for their nationalised firms and even in agriculture". (Ibid., p.7). Taylor in his review of the post-socialist transition from a global development economics point of view was basically arguing that the Indians had switched sectors and sub-sectors successfully from firm level controls to a sectoral level efficiency policy, linked with economy level strategic objectives. "The Theory of a Multi-Faceted Price System" advocated the perception that in the transitional stage, dual pricing, threat of imports and set-off could all be used, for limited periods of time, in such a policy regime. In this context M.J. Manohar Rao, for example shows that interest rate policy would have limited relevance in some periods of the Indian economic reform. If the influence of market economics is to be modelled in such an economy, the impact of market prices will have to be examined only in those sectors where the market was functioning. In the agricultural sector it was the food grain economy in which the State intervened effectively by price setting and quantitative interventions in purchases and sales. This part of the agricultural economy would therefore, be required to be modelled in an autonomous framework determined by a policy structure. The rest of the agricultural economy could be considered for an endogenous market determined framework.

In the nineties, interest revives in the issue of aggregate supply response and Mishra and Hazell (1996), covering the period 1952/53-1988/89, estimate the following equation:

$$1)\quad Q = \underset{(18332.69)}{-1940.29} + \underset{(75.56)}{114.11}\,TOT + \underset{(110.63)}{240.83}\,A + \underset{(6.25)}{2011.67}\,H$$

$$R^2 = 92.33$$

Where

Q = Agricultural output at 1980/81 prices

TOT = Gross terms of trade, 3 year moving average

A = gross cropped area (hectares)

H = % area under high yielding variety.

Standard errors in parentheses.

They find interaction between TOT and HYV of -13.97 significant at 5 per cent level. This shows that the Mishra-Hazell study results were bedeviled with multicollinearity, a problem of time series analysis of aggregate supply studies, which we discuss in detail later.

They conclude, "It seems that when important variables are included in the equation, the terms of trade seem to be moving in broad correspondence with the output changes over the period. *In view of 15 per cent level of significance, an inference about its positive impact on output would be rather difficult to draw, however.*" (Ibid., p.104, italics added). They are not price responsiveness pessimists but their empirical evidence leads them to a nebulous position. Also, Mishra and Hazell examine these relations together with rural poverty and private and public investment, which complicates matters. While Equation 1 was using OLS, later work was in a simultaneously determined framework (Mishra and Hazell, 1996).

Modelling Agricultural Supply

It is interesting that while in the traditional debates Indian economists took strong positions on price elasticity of aggregate supply response, there was recognition of the alternate position. Therefore, Chakravarty is emphatic in saying that, "It should be clearly recognized that in our context, agriculture cannot be treated as a bargain sector in the sense that its output can be increased with very little extra investment." (Chakravarti, 1969: 231) and again "a certain balance must be struck between the rates of growth of agriculture and the rest of the economy. An indispensable criterion for achieving a similar balance is that there cannot be a one way transfer of resources only." (Ibid., p.231). Raj Krishna as we saw sets prices functioning only in a favourable techno-economic episode and in the context of functioning market infrastructure. There is also the point made earlier that the relevant prices used as incentive signallers may change in long periods as decades. (Askari and Cummings, 1977, referred to above). This would then be the argument for modelling the stages of the policy and market development framework in the agricultural supply response debate.

Given this flavour of the debate and in the context of the wider developments in the Indian economy, which we have noted but do not review here, we postulate that:

a) price responsiveness does not determine supply expansion in the first traditional phase of Indian agriculture after Independence (the period 1950/1980) and that in this phase the main drivers of growth were area and technology;

b) in the period since then (1980 through the nineties), price incentives determine the aggregate effort the farmer puts in the agricultural system, for those aspects of the economy in which price incentives are allowed to function and in this context the application by the farmer, from the choices available to him of technology determines the supply outcomes; and

c) for the food grains economy, which was dominated by government policy objectives, the economy has to be modelled in the framework of an autonomous policy regime.

The analytical technique to be used for a) and b) will be an acreage response function and the derivation of a supply function plugging in a productivity relationship; c) Will be modelled separately in a non-behaviouristic mould.

As we have seen in the previous section the available estimates suggest an inelastic aggregate supply function with respect to prices, although supplies of individual crops are elastic to prices. Farmers' expectations of future relative prices play a role in shaping their decisions as to how many acres to devote to each crop. Why have low elasticities of acreage to deflated price been obtained? Studies suggest that farmers respond very little to price in planning their acreage. Individual farmers can and do shift when conditions made a shift profitable. This fact suggests that here may be substantial response to price in the production of individual crops. Thus, Bhagwati and Chakravarty (1969) state, "From certain economic points of view, the supply of the marketed surplus of direct wage-goods such as food-grains may be crucial but the supply of the surplus of overall agricultural produce may not be." (p. 37). High elasticities of substitution on individual farms do not, however, necessarily entail a high elasticity of supply for the industry as a whole. The extent of change of relative price may have to be very great before any substantial number of farms will shift. Farmers react, not to last year's price but rather to the price they expect, and this expected price depends only to a limited extent in what last year's price was.

Bapna (1980) estimates inelastic aggregate supply for the agricultural sector. Raj Krishna (1967) estimates elastic price responses to crops. Sawant (1978) estimates inelastic supply responses to individual crops in the pre war period and elastic supply responses in the post-war period. As contrasted with these results we hypothesise that the aggregate supply function for the agricultural sector is price elastic in the reform period of the Indian economy. Second, price elasticity estimates are statistically more significant after the appropriate lags are introduced. These hypotheses are empirically validated below.

Nerlove considers farmers' expectation of future relative prices in shaping their acreage decisions and he obtains higher elasticities for individual crops like corn, cotton and wheat in the USA (Nerlove, 1969). Behrman (1968) has not estimated aggregate supply response. His study concentrates upon the response to price changes of four major annual crops in Thailand during the period 1937-1967 at the Chorguard or provincial level. The results of the study strongly support the hypothesis that farmers in economically underdeveloped countries respond significantly and substantially to economic incentives. Raj Krishna (1962, 1963) also estimates elasticities of supply of crops and estimated the parameters of several supply relation of agricultural commodities in the Punjab region before 1946. Raj Krishna concludes that by correctly specifying the relevant non-price variables one can obtain significant net regression coefficient and elasticities of the price variable.

There has been a lot of work in recent periods on modified versions of the Nerlovian models described earlier. These include more systematic use of variance analysis to model uncertainty, search for systematic techniques to capture the exact nature of lags and integration of the work with speculation, futures markets and arbitrage (See, Antonovitz and Green, 1990; Leuthold, Julius and Cordier, 1990 and Wilson and Fung, 1991).

The Nerlovian models for acreage response can be stated now for the acreage response function is well known and can be derived as we saw in two different ways which are as follows:

(2) $P_t^* - P_{t-1}^* = b(P_{t-1} - P_{t-1}^*)$

where P is price, the superscript * stands for expected value, t is the subscript for time and $0<b<1$.

Let a_0 be a constant, b_1 a slope coefficient and e the random residual term. Then we can write the acreage response function as

(3) $A_t=a_0+b_1P_t^*+e_t$

According to (2), P_t^* is a function of P_{t-1} and P_{t-1}^*.

According to (3) P_t^* can be expressed as a function of A_t and P_{t-1}^* can be expressed as a function of A_{t-1}.

Therefore, P_t^* is a function of P_{t-1} and A_{t-1}. So in (3) we can substitute for P_t^* and obtain

(4) $A_t=a_1+b_2P_{t-1}+b_3A_{t-1}+e_t$.

The model in (4) can be specified further.

Nerlove provides two alternate theories. The first is the rigidity model. Suppose that P_t determines A_t^*, the desired A_t:

(4a) $A_t^* = b_4P_t$

However, the adjustment to the desired value is gradual, say on account of a credit constraint:

(4b) $A_t - A_{t-1}=d\ (A_t^*-A_{t-1})$

where $0<d<1$ is the coefficient of adjustment.

Inserting (4a) into (4b) and rewriting gives a variant of (4):

(5) $A_t = b_4d\ P_t-1+(1-d)\ A_t-1(6)$

The second is the expectation model. Suppose the expected value of P_{t+1} is P_t^* and this expected price determines acreage or A_t:

(4c) $A_t = b_4\ P_t^*$

However expectations of prices are formed recursively as follows:

(4d) $P_t^*= P_{t-1}^* + d(P_t - P_{t-1}^*)$

where $0<d<1$ is now the coefficient of expectation. Inserting (4d) into (4c), we get

(6) $A_t = b_4d\ P_t+ b_4(1-d)\ P_{t-1}^*$

$= b_4 d\ P_t + (1\text{-}d)\ A_{t\text{-}1}$

Since $P_{t\text{-}1}{}^{*} = 1/\ b_4\ A_{t\text{-}1}$ as a one year lagged version of (4c).

From an acreage response function, let us derive a supply response function. In the simplest case the series A_t on acreage in period 1,2,..............,t can be multiplied by Q_{ts}/A_t where Q_s stands for output, set exogenously every time period, and therefore, Qs/A is the productivity or output per acre of land. Substituting the Q_s/A variable in (4) for the A variable, will give us:

(7) $Q_{ts} = b_4 d\ P_t + b_4\ (1\text{-}d) Q_{st\text{-}1}$

Alternately the Q_{ts}/A variable can be estimated endogenously.

Data Sources and Trends

Index numbers of area and production of all crops, food grains and non-food grains are as estimated by the Directorate of Economics and Statistics of the Department of Agriculture and Cooperation of the Ministry of Agriculture, Government of India (DESA). Net and gross irrigated area are also taken from the land use statistics released from the same source. Fertiliser consumption statistics are from the Fertiliser Association of India. All these estimates are presented in *Agricultural Statistics at a Glance*, published by the DESA. Terms of Trade data are taken from two sources. The first is the implied price deflators in *National Account Statistics*, published by the Central Statistical Organisation. Gross value of output in the agricultural sector at current prices divided by the gross value of output in the agricultural sector at constant prices gives the price deflator for the agricultural sector. A similar procedure gives estimates for the non-agricultural sector. The ratio of the two estimates of price deflators gives the terms of trade for the agricultural sector (TOTn). The other source of this variable is the Reports of the Commission on Agricultural Costs and Prices, which prepares and publishes the Index of Terms of Trade between the agricultural and non-agricultural sectors (TOTc).

Results

To commence the analysis we have tested, as defined earlier

(4) $A_t = a_0 + b_5 P_{t-1} + e_t$

We first estimate this equation for the entire agricultural sector i.e., all crops for the entire period 1950/51-2003/04. The hypothesis is that the price variable is insignificant.

The results are as follows: (the figures in the brackets in all equations are standard errors):

(8) $A_t = 105 - 8.958\ TOT_{nt-1}$

(10.0) (9.87)

$R^2 = .016$ d.f=51

D.W = 0.15 Adj-R^2 = 0.003

The variable A as defined earlier is acreage under all crops, TOT_n is terms of trade as estimated from *National Account Statistics* through the implicit price deflators (p.102) and t stands for time. TOT is therefore, used with a one year lag. Figures in brackets are standard errors.

The TOT_{nt-1} variable is insignificant. Also, there is evidence of serial correlation, since for 51 degrees of freedom and one independent variable the d_L value is 1.50. These are statistically poor results.

We corroborate the results of earlier scholars that the Nerlovian hypothesis does not work for the entire Indian agricultural sector for the entire period under study. India's aggregate supply function for agriculture is not price responsive.

Similar results are obtained if equation (4) is estimated without a lag as in equation (9)

(9) $A_t = 107.81 - 11.64\ TOT_{nt}$

(10.78) (10.47)

$R^2 = .02$ d.f = 52

DW = 0.12 Adj-R^2 = 0.004

Equations 8 to 9 are broadly in agreement with the kind of results obtained by S.L. Bapna, although his models are from micro data. The results reported by Mishra and Hazell also are in tandem, as reported in

Equation 1. The reasons on account of which Mishra and Hazell do not drop the HYV variable after a strong correlation between the two independent variables are not quite clear.

We may now proceed to test alternative models. One approach is to periodise the framework of analysis based on some a priori policy or analytic considerations. Recent work of a fairly systematic type suggests 1980/81 as the dividing line (Morris, 1997). Morris's statistical review of the year of the break in the hindu growth rate has been validated in recent years by Dani and Subramanian, 2004) and others (Panagariya, 2004). Higher growth rates and policy changes are the main reasons for the two epochs of the Indian economy being treated as different for structural analysis. We accept Morris's analysis and take the year 1980/81 as the divider for the period 1950/51 to 2003/04. The new periods of analysis become 1950/51 to 1980/81 and 1981/82 to 2003/04.

Equation 10 gives the results for the period 1950/51 to 1980/81.

(10) $A_t = 85.06 + 5.568\ TOT_{nt}$

(11.3) (10.66)

$R^2 = 0.009$ d.f = 29

DW= 0.14 Adj-R^2= 0.0248

The TOTn variable is insignificant and hence price responsiveness is not estimated as significant for the aggregate agricultural sector in this period. The d_L value is 1.12. This is the period in which, to use the description by Raj Krishna, the market and commercial infrastructure was still being built. (Lagged versions of these equations give similar results.)

We now analyse the period 1981/82 to 2003/04. The first set of tests are for the terms of trade variable with a lag. The results are reported in Equation 10.

(10) $A_t = 83.77 + 19.19\ TOT_{nt-1}$

(10.61) (10.81)

$R^2 = 0.14$ d.f = 20

DW= 1.29 Adj-R^2 = 0.074

These results give the kind of weak results Mishra and Hazell report, namely a weak relationship between acreage response and terms of trade. The d_u value for the Durbin Watson d statistic for one independent variable and 20 degrees of freedom at 0.01 level of significance is 1.15 and so there is no serial correlation. The results are much better than for the period 1950/51 to 1980/81 but given the low R^2 do not suggest a strong price-market orientation to the agricultural economy as a whole. Similar results are obtained when the TOT variable is tried without a lag in Equation 11.

$$(11)\ A_t = 88.47 + 14.33\ TOT_{nt}$$

$$(10.03)\quad (10.46)$$

$R^2 = 0.08$ d.f.=21

DW=1.44 Adj-R^2=.033

The TOT variable is still not significant even at the 10 per cent level. For 21 degrees of freedom, the d_u value is 1.16, so there is no serial correlation.

We now test the postulate (b) above. This is based on the hypothesis that price signals activate a supply response in that part of the agricultural economy, which is allowed to adjust to price stimuli in a competitive economy. We postulate this is the non-food grain segment of the agricultural economy. It may be recalled that at the crop level price responsiveness has been estimated as statistically significant by various scholars. Our hypothesis is more general. It is that in a significant section of the agricultural economy, price signals determine supply response. Does this mean that the agricultural economy is now price responsive as a whole? This is a difficult question to answer in a transitional policy regime. (Mungekar, 1992; 1993). Most certainly the price responsive economy is growing faster. Whether it is on account of resource diversion or resource augmentation, needs are to be examined more closely. But first the results may be seen.

In the period since 1981/82 we postulate that acreage under non-food grains N is determined by the price of non-food grains, P_n. Since value of output data in current and constant prices is available in

National Account Statistics, we estimate P_n as the appropriate price deflator. Equation 12 gives the result.

$$(12)\quad N_t = 96.62+23.3\, P_{nt}$$

$$(3.03)\ (3.06)$$

$R^2=0.76$ d.f.=18

DW=1.52 Adj-R^2=.7501

It can be seen that in the reform period acreage response to prices in the non-food grains sector, which is market determined is highly price responsive. Unfortunately the disaggregated data at comparable prices for value of output is only available upto 1999/2000. This limits the degrees of freedom for inference. With 18 degrees of freedom, the value of d_u is 1.12 and so there is no serial correlation.

Equation 12 was estimated with a one year lag in the price variable. The results are as follows:

$$(13)\quad N_t = 99.59+21.79\, P_{nt-1}$$

$$(3.56)\quad (3.73)$$

$R^2=0.66$ d.f.=17

DW=1.60 Adj-R^2=0.65

The lagged response of acreage to prices is highly significant. The d_u value for 17 degrees of freedom is 1.10 and so there is no evidence of serial correlation.

The difficulty with Equations 12 and 13 is that the price variable is not a relative price variable. There is a more basic difficulty since a relative price variable for the non-food grains sector is not easily available. While prices received by the non-food grains sector are known, for example the P_n variable in Equations 12 and 13, there are no estimates of prices paid by the non-food grain sector. Thus, there is a problem in constructing a relative price variable for the non-food grain sector to test the stated hypothesis. In fact it has been argued that using crude relative variables in a two sector economy can lead to substantial specification errors (CSO, 1984: Appendix VII).

Economic analysis can suggest a way out. It can be reasonably argued that the economic environment for a farmer is broadly the same, whether he grows food grains or non-food grains. It is just that the actual stimuli he receives will depend on the intervention of the Government also. If this interpretation is correct then the economy level terms of trade or relative price variable will determine the acreage choice for those segments of the economy where the farmer operates in a market environment. In our notation this would imply that the N variable will be determined by the TOT variables. Before testing this hypothesis we decided to see if there was general congruence between different price variables affecting the agricultural sector. If P_f is the price of food grains variable, its relation with P_n could be examined. This was done in an earlier published work by the author (Alagh, 2004). The results were as follows (sample from 1980-81 to 1993-94 was taken for testing):

$$(14)\ P_n = \underset{(0.06)}{0.07} + \underset{(0.04)}{0.94}\ P_f$$

$R^2=0.98$ d.f.=12

Therefore, like many price series, the two prices move together. We also examined the relation between P_n and the aggregate price deflator for the agricultural sector as a whole. We defined this as P_a which is the price level of prices received by the agricultural sector as a whole. The relationship was seen to be as follows:

$$(15)\ P_n = \underset{(0.03)}{-0.03} + \underset{(0.02)}{1.03} P_a$$

$R^2=0.99$ d.f.=12

While prices tend to move together on account of macro relations, say with money supply, we consider this result an endorsement of the analytical position that the non-food grain sector is operating in an overall economic environment, which needs macro level analysis. It is to this that we now turn. The acreage response relations that we have been estimating are now estimated for the non-food grains sector but postulating that for resource allocation to that sector the farmer operates in the macro economy for the agricultural sector as a whole, in other words he responds to the agricultural terms of trade. The estimates are reported as follows:

(16)N_t=-55.66+177.03 TOT_{nt}

(24.26) (23.91)

R^2 = 0.71 d.f.= 21

DW = 0.82 Adj-R^2 = 0.61

Figures in brackets are standard errors.

The period is 1981-82 to 2003-04. Terms of trade determine acreage response in the non-food grains sector. The d_L value at 0.01 and 0.015 levels are 0.98 and 0.74 and so with an estimated value of the d statistic of 0.82 the inference on serial correlation is inconclusive in this variant of the estimate.

A log lin version of (16) is as follows:

(17) log N_t= log 26.49+4.56 TOT_n

(0.21) (0.21)

R^2 = 0.71 d.f. =21

D.W.=0.83 Adj-R^2 = 0.61

In a log lin regression elasticity b is multiplied by X. If the TOT is 1 or terms of trade are in parity, the elasticity of acreage response in Equation 17 is 4.56. This is high. The evidence on serial correlation is as in the last equation, inconclusive. There is evidence that the Indian farmer responds to a favourable environment for the market determined sector of the agricultural economy.

The double log version of this equation is as follows:

(18) log $N_{t\,=}$ log 4.58 - log 0.35TOT_{nt}

(0.86) (0.51)

R^2=0.43 d.f.=22

DW=1.67 Adj R^2=0.41

The regression is not significant but there is no serial correlation.

We now estimate the lagged specification of (16), (17) and (18). The results are as follows:

(19) $N_t = -49.85 + 172.37\ TOT_{nt-1}$

(26.33) (26.81)

$R^2 = 0.67$ d.f.=20

DW=0.43 Adj-$R^2 = 0.48$

(20) $\log N_t = \log 27.80425 + 4.389\ TOT_{nt-1}$

(0.23) (0.23)

$R^2 = 0.67$ d.f. =20

DW=0.62 Adj- $R^2 = 0.47$

The acreage response function is highly elastic to lagged prices with an elasticity of around 4.4 and the relationship is significant. But there is serial correlation.

The double log version is as follows:

(21) $\log N_t = \log 4.79 + 1.35 \log TOT_{nt-1}$

(0.02) (0.39)

$R^2 = 0.50$ d.f.= 22

DW=0.62 Adj $R^2 = 0.47$

The regression is significant, the elasticity of 1.35 is acceptable but there is serial correlation.

We again note that if a recursive system as a cobweb is specified say in two equations, as shown above: "The first equation may be estimated consistently by OLS." And again, "Thus an OLS regression of y_2 on y_1 and x will yield consistent estimates of the second structural equation." (Johnston, 1984: 468). Thus, the problem of serial correlation can be solved in the OLS structure by proper specification and data selection.

This behaviour is estimated for the period 1981 onwards. For the period 1950/51 to 1980-81 and for the entire period 1950/51 to 2003-04, the price elasticity of acreage response is insignificant and there is strong serial correlation, as the following estimates show:

For 1950-51/1980-81

(22) $N_t = 78.5+7.88\ TOT_{nt}$

(14.72) (13.88)

$R^2 = 0.01$ d.f.=29

DW = 0.15 Adj-$R^2 = 0.02$

For 1950-51 / 2003-04

(23) $N_t=121.43 - 20.63\ TOT_{nt}$

(25.22) (24.5)

$R^2= 0.01$ d.f.=52

DW = 0.04 Adj-$R^2 = 0.06$

(24) $N_t= 93.53 - 2.88\ TOT_{t-1}$

(1.02) (1.46)

$R^2=0.07$ d.f.=51

DW=.05 Adj-$R^2 = 0.001$

Robust Data and Estimated Values

The main results obtained are now estimated with more robust data. As is well known, the use of NAS terms of trade data for drawing inferences incentives or disincentives for the agricultural sector is strongly contested by agricultural economists. (In this connection, the standard text is Kahlon and Tyagi, 1983.) Following these critiques, separate terms of trade are worked out by the CACP by using the appropriate weights of purchases and sales of the agricultural sector. These estimates of relative prices of the agricultural sector with the non-agricultural sector are more robust and give us the proper indications of the economic environment faced by the agricultural sector. We now estimate the acreage response by using the terms of trade variable from the CACP estimates of the terms of trade for the agricultural sector (TOT_c).

For the period 1981-82 to 1999-2000

(25) $N_t=-84.11+2.02\ TOT_{ct}$

(25.31) (.25)

$R^2 = 0.78$ d.f. = 17

DW = 0.75 Adj-$R^2 = 0.78$

Using the log lin form, we get

(26) Log N_t = 20.53+1.01 TOT_{ct}

(0.21) (0.002)

R^2=.79 d.f.=17

DW= 0.75 Adj-R^2= 0.79

The elasticity of acreage response is now reasonable at 1.01, instead of 4.56, when the GDP deflator terms of trade were used. For 17 degrees of freedom at 0.015 levels of significance, we get an inconclusive value of the d statistic.

For the double log formulation we get:

(27) logN_t = log -3.08 + log 1.71 TOT_{ct}

(0.97) (0.21)

$R^2 = 0.79$ d.f. = 17

DW= 0.72 Adj R^2=0.78

The regression is significant, the elasticity is acceptable but the test of serial correlation is inconclusive.

The lagged estimate for this equation which is our theoretical specification, for this period was as follows:

(28) N_t= -86.17 + 2.05 TOT_{ct-1}

(21.13) (0.21)

R^2=0.85 d.f.=16

DW=1.16 Adj-R^2= 0.85

The regression is highly significant and the required d_u value is 1.10, so there is no evidence of serial correlation.

The log lin estimates and the double log estimates for this are as follows and confirm the results:

(29) Log N_t= 20.23+1.01 TOT_{ct-1}

(0.177) (0.002)

$R^2 = 0.86$ d.f. =16

DW= 1.16 Adj-R^2 = 0.4718

(30) $\log N_t = \log -3.21 + 1.74 \log TOT_{ct-1}$

(0.81) (0.18)

$R^2 = 0.86$ d.f.= 16

DW= 1.09 Adj R^2 = 0.85

These are our reference results and strongly validate our theoretical hypotheses. The estimated equations are statistically significant and do not have serial correlation. The latter result emerges for this set of equations as compared to the *National Account Statistics* terms of trade, we believe, because the Commission of Agricultural Costs and Prices Terms of Trade is more robust in depicting the economic reality faced by the farm sector.

The Supply Function

We postulate that the aggregate supply function for Indian agriculture would in the light of the above analysis consist of a price responsive non-food grains sector and a trend determined food grains sector with the farmer confident that government determined prices for grain would rise as in the past. The non-food grains supply function is recursively determined. This kind of relation is associated with H. Wold's work (See a simplified description in Carl Christ, (1966: 454-456). The first decision the farmer makes in the light of market trends is to allocate land resources to non-food grains. After that from the available technologies, he choses his input basket. This system could be specified as follows:

(31) $\log N_t = a_1 + b_1 \log TOT_{t-1} + \log u_t$

Definitionally output (Q_n = Output in the non-food grains sector) equals area times productivity of land. Productivity of land in the simplest case can be determined with a time trend as in the Solow technical change sense. Thus:

(32) $\log Q_{nt}/N_t = a_2 + b_{2t} + u_t$

Substituting (23) in (24) will give us the supply function:

(33) $\log Q_{nt} = a_o + b\log TOT_{t-1} + c_t$

In (33) a_o and b are linear combinations of the variables in (31) and (32). Acreage will be determined by the Nerlovian relation and productivity by technical change. These estimates are presented in the next chapter. Since for forecasting purposes the regression period will have to end at 1995, since the period after that will be the forecast period, we decided to test the relation 31 for the period 1980/81 to 1995/96. The double log equation is estimated as follows:

(34) $\log N_t = \log 3.01 + 1.77 \log TOT_{ct-1}$

(0.17) (0.17)

$R^2 = 0.86$ d.f.16

DW= 1.16 Adj $R^2 = 0.85$

The regression is significant and there is no serial correlation. We will use alternate functional forms in the next chapter for forecasting but the theoretical foundation is empirically valid.

Conclusion

It is not quite correct to say that Indian agriculture responds at the aggregate level to price stimuli. The agrarian economy reflects the transitional nature of the policy regime since 1980. It is now quite clear that allocation of land resources to non-food grain crops is price elastic. We believe this result is more substantive than the statement that at the crop level resource allocation was price sensitive, which has been accepted for long as our review shows. In the light of these results, ignoring the marketisation of substantial sections of the economy will create both an understanding and a policy problem. We developed in this chapter an appropriate system which explains developments and is also a tool in the transitional regime. We use it for policy analysis, both of a forecasting nature as also of a normative welfare gains type in the next chapter. Not having the resources of large research bodies or policy setting agencies, our analysis is preliminary and of an illustrative nature and only demonstrates the possibilities of this kind of work.

4 Policy Analysis

Introduction

Policy analysis in economics has a specific context; developed by great economists, like the first economics Nobel Laureate Jan Tinbergen, it has a technical core.

Positive economic analysis explains economic phenomenon. Dependent variables like income, employment or prices can be explained by independent variables like aggregate demand, micro demand and supply schedules, given the structure of the relationship between the dependent and independent variables. For economic policy analysis Tinbergen turned the causal arrows around. Given the normatively set policy objectives, the attempt of policy analysis was to find out if possible policy configurations existed, given the structure of economic relationships and the policy instruments available. There were two objectives. First to see if a feasible instrumental set existed for the preferred policies and if it did, then second to determine what it was (Tinbergen, 1956). The Tinbergen Theory of Economic Policy would, therefore, like us to build an analytical frame where we go from objectives through the structure to the instruments to be worked on.

In this chapter, we first explain the traditional theory of economic policy in a simple fashion. This is based on the work of Tinbergen (1956) and we describe and outline the characteristics of policy models, namely the derivation of feasible and optimal policy sets in a system in which objectives are given, the structure of the economy is estimated and given the objectives, the policy instruments are worked out. In the next section, we review some of the policy literature, both at home and abroad. In India, in the early nineties the contours of the problems the country was to face, namely the continuation of the agricultural growth and diversification process in the eighties together with meeting food security objectives was foreseen in some detail by scholars. Indian studies anticipated that in a distorted global agricultural economy, reliance only on market instruments could lead to volatility and slowing down both of agricultural growth and diversification. Again reliance on trade could lead to excessive costs in meeting food security objectives given the size of the Indian food requirements and imperfect competition in global food markets. On the other hand, it was also very clear that continuation of controls and excessive quantitative interventions would be counterproductive. The requirement was, therefore, of developing transitional policies, using both markets and State level strategic guidance. In contrast, in the global literature there was a much greater reliance on open economy agricultural trade models. We outline these themes in India and abroad. In the final section, we give two applications of the tools developed in this work. We use the cobweb models developed in Chapter 3 to see if we can forecast aggregate non-food grain acreages and supply in India. We are able to demonstrate through the use of our models that market determined econometric models forecast the swings of the commercial non-food grains section of the agricultural economy of India. The fact that the models track the agricultural cycle is, we believe, a justification of the work done. However, we are not able to track with great accuracy the exact dimensions of the cyclical swings. At the end of this chapter, having established in earlier chapters that market stimuli work in non-food grain sectors, we use a partial equilibrium analytical framework to work out the impact of market instruments like tariff policies and domestic price interventions in the cotton crop. We work out the welfare impact of trade interventions and find that given the imperfect nature of policies, policy interventions transfer welfare to producers in the country from which imports to India are sourced, and there is a small gain in welfare to Indian consumers. This simulation anticipates recent Indian experience in Indian food imports, where imports have been made at prices higher than in Indian markets and later subsidised.

Review of Policy Literature

The Theory of Economic Policy

Jan Tinbergen begins his analysis of economic policy by explaining "Economic Policy consists in the deliberate variation in means in order to attain certain aims" (Tinbergen, 1956: xi). He further says, "According to the nature of means involved, policy maybe "reform" (change in foundations) "qualitative policy" (change in structure) or "quantitative policy"(change only in value of instrument variables)" (Ibid.: xii).

We are interested in quantitative policy, being mainly directed towards a change in the numerical values of some of the economic variables, to be called targets.

"Basic for all discussions—and discussions on economic policy are no exceptions to this rule—is a clear and precise setting out of the problems to be discussed" (Ibid.: 1).

He begins by defining data "The given elements are called "data", they refer to the natural, technical, psychological, institutional and international elements which the economic action of man has to take for granted. Examples are climate, the crops, technical processes, human preferences, habits, laws, political agreements, world market prices and world-market demand" (Ibid.: 3).

Tinbergen further writes, "The elements of economic action itself will be indicated as "economic phenomena", their quantitative aspects also as "economic variables", examples are volume of production, prices, income, expenditures, capital etc. They are supposed to be logically explicable in terms of the data" (Ibid.: 3).

He describes data as, "Among the data there are some that can be changed—to a greater or a lesser degree—by policy makers. They will be called "means" of economic policy; those that cannot be changed by policy makers are called the "other data" (Ibid.: 4).

He defines structure as, "The quantitative elements may be exemplified by the number of social groups and institutions, their behaviour (e.g. their demand elasticities or their propensities to consume), the number of goods handled or the quantitative composition of an economys real wealth." And instruments "There remains the class of means, which as a rule, are of a quantitative character and are used for frequent changes, in fact for the adaptation of the economy to small and frequent changes in some of the other data. This class will be called "instruments" or "instrument variables" and may be exemplified by tax rates, items of public expenditure, the rates of discount reserve ratios and foreign exchange rates" (Ibid., p.5).

The problem of policy is to work out the values of instruments required to meet objectives, given the data or structure.

Some Indian Approaches

We saw the statist approach to agricultural policies in India, with many scholars bringing in a considerable degree of market understanding (Ch.1). The works of well known scholars like Prof. Dantwala, Hanumantha Rao, Dr. Kahlon and Tyagi were reviewed in that context. According to S.S. Acharya, as we saw earlier (Ch.1), the Government has an important role to play in agricultural markets since there were many reasons of market failure, particularly in developing economies. In countries where average incomes are high, markets well developed, government revenue high, a small proportion of the population depends on agriculture and supply response to price changes is high, intervention lays emphasis on providing income support to farmers.

In less developed countries where the agricultural sector accounts for the lion's share of gross national product, a large proportion of population depends on agriculture and markets are not well developed, the emphasis is on encouraging production to meet the growing demand and making available basic food to all sections of society at affordable prices.

Government intervention in pricing of farm products has taken various forms like price support, procurement of farm products, maintenance of buffer stocks, restriction on the movement of products, regulation of imports and exports and restrictions on the activities of traders.

The forms of intervention can be grouped under the following broad heads:

- Administered prices.
- Influencing supply and demand.
- Influencing the behaviour of market functionaries and creation of market infrastructural facilities.

In the nineties, other formulations on policy structures in developing economies questioned the role of the State, once the agricultural economy gained in depth and size. D.S. Tyagi in a study on the managing of the food policy in India starts by saying that the most significant achievement of this policy was been a substantial increase in the economic and physical access to food. The fact that the food policy was successful in effectively tackling the problems arising out of droughts was significant. "As a consequence of Government intervention in the marketing of food grains, the degree of exploitation by the trade both of producers and consumers has been substantially reduced" (Tyagi, 1990: 13). However, he also brings out limitations "Despite an extensive public distribution programme, the benefits have quite often not reached the most vulnerable sections of society. On the producers' side also, it is the more vulnerable section of producers growing rainfed crops like *jowar*, *bajra* and maize that has failed to benefit from the Government policy of assuring a remunerative price" (Ibid.: 13).

D.S. Tyagi was one of the earlier economists to outline new problems emerging as a consequence of increased intervention by the government agencies in domestic trade and India emerging as a marginally self-sufficient economy in cereals. "Market arrivals are increasingly concentrated only to a few weeks period. Because of increasing transportation, storage and handling charges, the difference between the cost at which the public sector agencies can distribute food grains without subsidy (the economic cost) and the producer price is becoming wider year after year. As a consequence the difference between the economic cost and the issue price is becoming larger" (Ibid.: 13).

Going back to policy origins, he says, "Thus, it is evident from the above that one of the main considerations that had forced various committees to recommend and the Government to intervene in the marketing of food grains was the fear that in a period of scarcity, given the inelastic nature of the demand for food grains and the vast differences in the purchasing power of different communities/regions, an unhampered play of free market forces would result in a situation where food grains would not be within the reach of many communities/areas as prices may rise steeply. If one were to agree that in the coming decade the food grains supplies from the domestic production in India are going to match the domestic demand, then at least on the above ground of 'scarcity' there is no case for the continuation of controls." However, in a sense anticipating recent history, "notwithstanding the contention that India would emerge as a completely self-sufficient economy in the near future, the possibilities of food grain prices displaying large intra- and inter-year fluctuations cannot be ruled out" (Ibid.: 172).

More than a decade ago, D.S. Tyagi foresaw the crisis of 2006. "It needs to be noted that when the prices of wheat were high in the domestic market, even if the government would have allowed free trade in wheat and other cereals no net import would have taken place. This would have happened even in years when the world market prices were lower than the domestic market prices as the landed cost of food grains would have been much higher than the prevailing prices in the domestic market. Similarly when the world market prices were lower than the domestic market prices despite there being an excess supply in the country no net export of wheat or rice would have taken place. Thus the operations of private trade through the use of the world market would not have been in a position to bring about the desired supply-demand balance" (Ibid.: 175).

The world agricultural market was highly volatile. The fact that a large part of the per capita income in India is spent on food would suggest that such large fluctuations cannot be absorbed in the Indian economy without serious repercussions. Thus, even in a self-sufficient environment with no restrictions on trade, the problem of high fluctuations in domestic prices would remain. D.S. Tyagi's empathy for the analytical masters of India's agricultural economy shows in his stress on the prices of food grains in the Indian situation not being detached from the paying capacity of the large mass of low income consumers. Any substantial increase in the price of basic food grains would reduce the entitlement of many consumers quite substantially. This reduction in their entitlement may even lead to starvation. On the other hand, very low prices for food grains may lead to the deterioration of the economic condition of farmers to such an extent that investment in the farm sector may suffer a serious setback. Thus, the Government is faced with the task of keeping the prices of food grains within certain limits both from the point of view of producers and consumers. This in turn requires that the balance between the supply and demand for different food grains is to be maintained.

It was evident from his discussion that an unrestricted trade policy both for the domestic as well as the world market would not solve the problem of the large fluctuations in prices. Traditional welfare economists often conclude that commodity price stabilisation schemes are economically wasteful. Such conclusions are based on the logic that a rational consumer can save when prices are low, thereby enabling him to purchase when prices are high, thus on an average he is better off with price instability. However, in reality this does not happen where the level of poverty is high and capital markets are imperfect. Tyagi quotes earlier field studies to argue that an unsatiated consumer cannot hold back on consumption sufficiently during a low price season. He cannot plan with a time horizon that includes a two price situation, and therefore an average of the two situations is not applicable to him (Ahmed and Andrew, 1989: 78). A study by Jodha (1978) indicated that the drought affected population first reduces consumption, then defers committed obligations and reschedules current production activities. As the shock becomes more severe, they deplete inventories, livestock and utensils; mortgage or sell land; and finally migrate to urban centres or other areas. Price instability, therefore, has the potential for accelerating the process of pauperisation (Ahmed, 1989).

It can be suggested that instead of directly entering into the marketing of food grains, the Government should vary fiscal imposts on the imports and exports of food grains in such a manner as would keep the domestic supply and demand in balance. The highly volatile nature of the world market and the quantum of likely transactions would result in sharp fluctuations in the foreign exchange/subsidy outflows from the Government budget. As a summary to the system, prevailing when he was analysing it, Tyagi says, "In spite of the fact that the present system of managing India's food economy has paid rich dividends in the form of higher production, increased availability of cereals and increased economic access to food along with the effectively insulating the economy against the occurrence of famines even in the face of severe drought, it needs modification. The need for such modifications arises mainly because it has not succeeded in protecting the interests of the most vulnerable sections of the population whether amongst the consumers or among the producers. Further the role of the Government in the marketing of food grains is getting increasingly enlarged, as a consequence of which the subsidy bill has been expanding at a rapid rate without its benefit percolating to the poor. In certain cases this enlarged role has also tended to adversely affect the efficiency of the marketing system" (Tyagi, 1990: 181).

As discussed in our summary of Tyagi in the preceding paragraphs "...it is imperative for the Government to continue to intervene in the marketing of food grains." Tyagi notes that, "..the three main planks of Government's food policy are: a) ensuring the availability of cereals at reasonable prices to the consumers, particularly to the vulnerable sections of society, b) assurance of a remunerative price to the producer so that he can pursue his production efforts without the fear of prices declining to unremunerative levels even in the face of a glut, and c) given the nature of fluctuations in the output of food grains in the country, to hold a large buffer stock of food grains as a measure of security" (Ibid.: 181)

Tyagi makes the point that wheat and rice are available now to the consumers in the market at a relatively lower price than before. "Relatively speaking, the open market prices of these two cereals in real terms are much lower than was the case when a large part of the population was brought under the coverage of the public distribution programme." He concludes, "Therefore, a straight case exists for the Government to reduce its commitment of distribution of food grains to a large majority of the people now covered under the public distribution system." However, he adds, "No doubt, as far as the vulnerable sections are concerned, intervention by the Government must continue" (Ibid.: 183).

Price rise can be controlled effectively through operations at the wholesale level for this control over retail distribution is not necessary. A case in favour of continuing the present system of fair price shops with universal coverage is often made out on the grounds that if the general public distribution system is withdrawn and its operation is confined only to the most vulnerable sections of society, then in a year of drought it would be difficult to manage the food economy. In this context, it needs to be appreciated that distribution through the public distribution system has played a part in tackling the problem of scarcities in times of drought but other measures have helped more in solving the problem of hunger. Thus, a switchover from a system of universal entitlement to one restricted to the vulnerable sections together with a policy of open market sales at the wholesale level can effectively solve the problems of scarcity and rising prices in years of drought.

It is on account of arguments of the type D.S. Tyagi developed that we largely restrict our market response analysis and policy tools to the non-food grains economy. Also our emphasis is on prices as instruments and impacts of price policies.

The Macro Economy and Agricultural Policies in the Present Phase

We have seen with Prof. V.S. Vyas, in earlier chapters, the unfolding of underlying trends in Indian agriculture. But Vyas does not only explain the situation as it is, he also puts into focus the new challenges. "There are three important directions in which reforms in agricultural sector have been initiated. In the first place, restriction on the movement of food grains from one region to another has been removed. An all-India market in agriculture products has emerged, secondly, agricultural trade policy is liberalised, and exports are being encouraged. Indian agriculture is slowly but progressively getting integrated with the global economy. Thirdly, far reaching reforms have been introduced in the credit delivery systems. At the same time important producer and supportive measures e.g. rural poverty alleviation program, agricultural price support policies etc. have continued" (Vyas, 2003: 46).

Vyas has important implications for the future. "There are several important areas which warrant immediate attention. In the first place, the pace of agricultural growth will have to be accelerated significantly to meet the future requirements. On the basis of a careful study jointly conducted by the International Food Policy Research Institite and the Indian Agricultural Research Institute, demand for cereals for the year 2020 has been estimated at about 293 million tons as against present supply of around 180 million tons. The situation is further complicated as the demand for non cereal food is likely to increase much faster, as the consumption pattern both rural and urban areas is fast changing with higher weight being assigned to non cereal food" (Ibid.: 46). Thus he says, "The increasing demand for agricultural products has to be viewed in the context of a situation which suggests that we might have reached a plateau in agricultural production. The accelerated pace in agricultural production witnessed during the green revolution period is petering out. An important development in the past years was that the supply of the food grains and other agricultural products was enhanced at lower costs in the real terms because of improved technologies. However no such trend was observed in coarse cereals as the technological change in the production of these crops had been limited. Momentum of decline in the real cost of production has been halted in recent years. The total factor productivity growth, or the growth in the amount of output generated by a unit of inputs, seem to be declining. A question is seriously debated whether Indian agriculture has become high cost agriculture" (Ibid.: 46).

He elaborates, "The agrarian structure in the country has not changed much. Over a period of time there is a slight tilt in favour of the small holdings. Therefore in the ensuing period a substantial contribution to agricultural growth will have to come from small and medium holdings. There is enough evidence to suggest that given an easy access to productive inputs the small farmers also produce as efficiently in fact more efficiently than the large farmers. However, the critical factor is the access to resources, and among these resources availability of timely credit on fair terms is of critical importance. The institutions of input delivery, particularly those of credit delivery, are not yet attuned to serve the small farmers" (Ibid.: 47).

He brings into focus related problems. "There is the related problem of employment in the rural areas. It is quite clear that in foreseeable future we cannot expect a substantial withdrawal of labour force from farm to non-farm sectors. A very large number of existing households owning or cultivating small holding will continue to be attached to the land for their livelihood as well as employment. To improve their living as well as to enable them to cross the poverty line, which is one of the most important objectives of our national economic policy, creations of such conditions that the income of holdings improves satisfactorily should be given priority. In order to achieve this objective, one approach is to improve Total Factor Productivity (TFP) on these farms but that will not suffice.... For that it is necessary to introduce high value crops on these farms. Such a change in cropping pattern or enterprise mix would entail even greater reliance on modern inputs and therefore on credit" (Ibid., p.48).

Finally, a development that he raises which is as worrisome as the decline in TFP is the neglect and/or misuse of the natural resources i.e., land, water and forests. As a matter of fact, both these developments are interrelated. Degradation of natural resources leads to decline in TFP. And rejuvenation of natural resources could augment natural production and serve other objective such as employment generation. Soil conservation practices is one such example which strengthens production base and generates gainful employment.

Required new directions are listed out by Vyas as follows:

"It is clear that if the present trends continue and corrective steps are not taken the gains which we have accumulated during the last 25 years or so will be dissipated. He quotes the International Food Policy Research Institute—International Agricultural Research Institute projections which state that by 2020 we may end up with a surplus of 23 million tons in the cereals if present trends continue, or a surplus of about 20 million tons if we are able to raise the productivity" (Ibid., p.49). By way of explanation, this contra intuitive result emerges in the IFPRI/IARI study, since the productivity increase scenario is a normative scenario in which demand rises faster, and therefore, surpluses go down.

He also summarises other issues such as reducing subsidies, encouraging non-price factors such as technology, extension, research and development and increasing public capital formation.

Trade Liberalisation

G.S. Bhalla (2004) sets the stage by noting that earlier under General Agreement on Trade and Tariff (GATT), liberalisation of trade was mainly confined to trade in manufacturing. Despite several rounds of negotiations, GATT was unable to resolve the conflicting interests of the European Union and the United States of America on the issue of agricultural trade. The completion of the Uruguay Round of negotiations and the signing of the Agreement on Agriculture (AOA) in 1995 was a major achievement for trade liberalisation in agriculture and marks a new chapter in the history of multilateral trade negotiations.

The negotiations on agriculture resulted in four main provisions of the Agreement, the Agreement on Agriculture itself; the concessions and commitment Members are to undertake on market access, domestic support and export subsidies; the Agreement on Sanitary and Phyto-sanitary Measures; and the Ministerial Declaration concerning least developed and net food-importing developing countries.

The rationale for trade liberalisation was based on the assumption that a free multilateral trade regime leads to a significant increase in world trade and benefits all the trading partners. In particular, the developing countries were likely to specially benefit due to increased agricultural exports to developed countries because of their natural comparative advantage in agriculture subsequent to the envisaged withdrawal of domestic and export subsidies by the developed countries. But the main challenges for the developing countries would be to increase the efficiency of production and to create institutional mechanisms to enable the small and marginal farmers to share the benefits of agricultural diversification and increased agricultural exports. On the other hand, the opening of all barriers to agricultural trade was also likely to pose some critical challenges because of the possibility of large scale imports.

The arguments that trade benefits all the trading partners and also leads to maximisation of welfare are based on Ricardo's well known theory of comparative advantage. Another argument was that the import substitution strategy of industrialisation in the developing countries discriminated against tradeable agriculture. This happened because of several reasons including overvalued exchange rate, setting agricultural prices much below the border price for food security reasons, and restrictions on movement of agricultural commodities in general and food grains, in particular. All these led to lower realisation by the farmers.

Bhalla points out that "Several authors like Anderson and R. Tyres (1993), Cramer *et al.*, (1993), Evans and Walsh (1994), tried to make quantitative estimates of gains from trade liberalisation in agriculture by using elaborate global models. The general conclusion of these studies is that large quantitative gains would accrue to most of the developing countries, following withdrawal of subsidies by the developed countries. The authors also traced the effect of trade liberalisation and tariff reduction on changes in prices and incomes of exporting and importing countries. In this connection, reference may also be made to the Economic Survey, Government of India, 1994 and 1995 which predicted huge gains to the country from agricultural trade liberalisation" (Bhalla, 2004: 37).

However, he argues that, "A critical examination of these estimates shows that by and large, projected quantitative estimates of gains to various countries have not turned out to be correct. There can be many reasons for this. Firstly, in any global model the number of variables to be taken into account is very large, and it is difficult to estimate their relative movement. But more important, the assumption of the models that the developed countries would lower their tariffs and reduce subsidies has not proved correct" (Ibid.: 38).

Bhattacharyya, 2004, also largely agrees with this perspective. "In the history of global agricultural trade policy, 1995 is considered to be a watershed as the Agreement on Agriculture, negotiated under the Uruguay Round, came into effect that year. India, as a founder member of GATT, was also a party to this agreement. It was expected that the AOA would usher a new era of free and market-oriented agricultural trade and would be particularly beneficial to the developing countries.

However, India's agricultural trade performance since 1995 has not been satisfactory. India's agricultural export growth rate since 1995 has shown extreme volatility. After registering positive growth rates in 1995-1996 and 1996-97, agricultural exports from India showed negative growth rates for the next three years. In 2000-01, the growth rate has turned positive but the value of agricultural exports in 2000-01 was less than that of the year 1995-96.

Share of agriculture in total exports has gone down steadily in the post-1995 period. As against 19.2 per cent in 1995, agriculture in 2000-2001 contributed about 13.5 per cent of total exports in 2000-2001. India's agricultural imports have also displayed extreme fluctuations. The growth rate varied between (minus) 37 per cent and 64 per cent. The percentage share of agricultural imports in total imports has also shown high volatility. However, it is interesting to observe that in contrast to the a priori expectations, agricultural imports showed a negative rate of growth during 2000-2001, the first year when the impact of removal of QR on agricultural imports was supposed to have been felt" (Bhattacharyya, 2004: 51).

More recently there is more conservatism on postulating gains from trade. Thus, a recent World Bank study estimates that gains from trade liberalisation in agriculture will be $0.2 billion to India in the Doha Round at 2001 $ prices (Anderson and Martin (2005), Table 12.14 with SSPs {Special Safeguard Provisions}). On the other hand, as compared to a total gain of $2.2 billion, UNCTAD studies estimate that tariff losses to India will be $7.9 billion (Cordoba and Vanzetti, (2005), Table 11).

These kind of results have led Jagdish Bhagwati to suggest in media interviews (as reported in RIS Dairy, October 2006) that if poor countries that are dependent on tariff revenues for social spending risk losing those revenues by cutting tariffs, international agencies such as the World Bank should stand ready to make up the difference until their tax systems can be fixed to raise revenues in other, more appropriate, ways.

Some Recent Global Studies

A very rich literature is developing on some of these policy concerns on agricultural sectors on a global plane. Some of the dominant themes are analysis of risks and uncertainty, where the analysis is now not just of the Nerlovian approaches but use of instruments for reducing risk impacts. Policy impact studies which measure the outcomes of changes in instrumental variables is another field. Tariff and trade policy impacts are also studied. Finally, there is literature on welfare impacts of policies. We will briefly review some of the major studies, more to give a flavour of the methods used rather than a substantive discussion of each result and then follow the review with a forecast of our Nerlovian models to test their predictive capabilities and a welfare analysis of some recent policy instruments involving trade and domestic interventions.

Luther Tweeten (1989), examines policy issues in a broad sweep, macro-linkages, foreign trade, the efficiency of agriculture business and the more current agricultural issues relating to the environment, rural poverty, food safety and rural development. The book is a 'How to do it' manual. An interesting application of supply elasticies techniques is Adelaja (1991).

In India, the Commission on Agricultural Costs and Policies (Government of India, 2000) has modelled agricultural supply elasticity. Positive and significant supply elasticies were found for industrial crops contradictory to the notions of perversity of supply response to price. However, perverse supply response of total agricultural production cannot be rejected, they argue. It was believed that farmers do not allocate resources as guided by prices, marginal costs and returns conditions. However, various farms management studies showed that farmers do take prices and costs into account while allocating their scarce resources among various farms' enterprises indicated by the analysis of marginal costs and returns. Later, supply response studies have shown that farmers respond positively and significantly to prices and other economic incentives in allocating resources among different competing crops. Because of the positive and significant supply elasticities obtained for individual crops, it is now widely accepted that price policy is an effective instrument to achieve crop mix according to the targets which may be set in the plans. Can price policy be an effective tool for increasing aggregate production also, they ask? They say, most resources in agriculture are substitutable among crops, and therefore, farmers can shift resources according to the signals of price and profitability. But modelling of resources, the agricultural and non-agricultural sectors, is low, therefore, changes in overall resource may not be easy.

Leuthold, Raymond and Cordier (1990), integrate in some detail agricultural futures market with financial futures markets. Since this is an aspect under considerable discussion and emphasis in India these days, the present state of the art is seen in the development of institutions like the National Commodity Exchanges (NCDEX) with online trading which has led to newer perspectives. J. Lapp (1990) presents an imperfect info-rational expectations model of relative price determination. This model provides an econometric specification of testing for a causal relationship between money and the relative prices of agricultural commodities tax, results indicate that variations in the growth rate of nominal money supply whether anticipated or unanticipated have not been an important influence on the average level of price revealed by farmers relative to other prices in the economy over the period 1951-1985.

Uncertainty, as is well known from the analysis of user costs in the general theory leads to standard results not holding. A striking result in the theory of the competitive firm under certainly is the proposition that a proportional profits tax (with full offsets for losses) will have no impact on optimal output. This result does not apply under uncertainty. Quiggin (1991), Wilson and Fung (1991) show that many arbitrage opportunities have become available for market participants since the inception of trading in options. Central to many of these is the put-call parity relationship. If this condition is violated, arbitrage profits could be earned. Lapan *et al.*, 1991, analyse production, hedging and speculative decisions when both futures and options can be used in an expected utility model of price and basic uncertainty. When futures of option prices are unbiased optional hedging requires only futures and options can be used in an expected utility model of price and basis uncertainty. Tronstad and Taylor, 1991 utilise a stochastic dynamic programming (SDP) model that considers the state variables of: (a) before tax income, (b) grain storage, (c) quantity of futures position, (d) value of futures position, (e) wheat price, and (f) basic level.

Pick, 1990 opens up the analysis to a trading economy and analyses the effect of exchange rate risk of US agricultural trade flows, which underscores the importance of exchange rate risk in developing countries trade behaviour issues such as the establishment of well developed financial and commodity markets in developing countries. Pompelli and Pick 1990, follow through and examine the extent to which exchange rates and tariff changes are passed through the US import prices of unmanufactured tobacco from Brazil. Agricultural prices are not as flexible as commonly thought. Exchange rates and tariff changes are not fully passed through to the US tobacco import prices. Anania and Mclalla (1991), modelling discriminating trade policies, such as targeted embargoes or targeted subsidies argue that failure to explicitly include assumptions about the possibility of simultaneous exporting and importing may yield misleading results.

Conclusion

Policy analysis for the agricultural sector is becoming a very powerful tool all over the world. In India, the tradition is just beginning. Tools of introducing uncertainty into the understanding of the agricultural economy and policy analysis are now very common. Uncertainty meant the use of arbitrage, futures and hedging in price and stock-flow relationships. In the theoretical literature, there is a healthy mixture of well behaved neoclassical models with non-equilibriating models.

The nineties sees the emergence of market economics as a major explanation for agricultural analysis and advocacy for its use in policies in India. D.S. Tyagi was a major contributor in this regard, although his work also showed a healthy respect for market failure in poor countries, particularly on the relationship between agricultural prices, grain demand and food security.

The nineties also sees the introduction of open economy techniques in agricultural analysis. In the international literature, apart from general equilibrium models, there emerge studies of trade and its impact as also of trade instruments, including tariff and tax policies. Indian literature also takes cognizance of open economy implications, although it was largely critical of trade impacts.

These themes are important in this study. If market factors play a larger role in the farmer's economic decisions, then it is obvious that these should be used for policy analysis, for example forecasting exercises. Welfare to society will also be determined by economic policies like tariffs, domestic market restrictions, etc., so we work these out.

Policy Simulations

We attempt to illustrate our analysis of some empirical relationships in earlier chapters by stylised policy experiments. We use two experiments. The first is to use our work on the aggregate supply function to forecast supply of the non-food grains sub-sector of the Indian agricultural economy. It may be noted that as seen above, the Commission on Agricultural Costs and Prices has already stated that at the crop level these supply models would work. However, it is obvious that if they work at a more aggregative level, policy spaces of a more powerful kind would emerge in the transitional phase in which Indian economic policies are at the present stage. Therefore, our policy experiment will have some academic and policy interest. In the second example we would use the structure of classical welfare analysis to model gains and losses of the government intervention policies in an open economy in a partial equilibrium framework. There is a tradition in India of analysing policy impacts in a general equilibrium framework in the work of Prof. R. Radhakrishna and Indrakant (1988). However, that important work is not in an open economy framework. We look at import and trade effects but in a partial frame with all its limitations, which are spelt out.

Supply Projections

Acreage Projections with Acreage Response

We use the supply models developed for the non-food grains sector of the Indian agricultural economy in the last chapter. However, we need a different periodisation of the economy. It may be recalled that the acreage response curve is highly significant for the period 1980/81 to 2003/04 (Chapter 3, pp.114-115). However, better results are achieved when the terms of trade variable is estimated from CACP data. These estimates are available only upto 1999/2000. The results are as follows:

The lagged estimate for the period 1980/2000 was as follows:

$$(1) A_{nt} = -86.17 + 2.05\ TOT_{ct-1}$$

(21.13) (0.21)

R^2=0.85 d.f.=16

DW=0.75 Adj R^2=0.77

Here, A=Acreage; TOT= Terms of Trade; the subscripts $_{c,n,t,}$ stand for CACP data, non-food grains and time respectively. The figures in bracket are standard errors and DW is the Durbin Watson Statistic.

As seen in the last chapter, these results are statistically significant and for 17 degrees of freedom at 0.015 levels of significance, we get an inconclusive value of the d statistic.

The log lin estimates for this are as follows and confirm the results:

$$(2) \text{Log } A_{nt} = \log 20.23 + 1.01\ TOT_{ct-1}$$

(0.177) (0.002)

R^2=0.86 d.f. =16

DW = 1.16 Adj-R^2= 0.79

The elasticity of acreage response is now reasonable at 1.01 (in the log lin model elasticity is measured as product of beta coefficient and the independent or X variable so that with value of beta coefficient as 1.01 and the independent variable the Terms of Trade assumed to be one we get the value of 1.01) as required by Nerlovain theory instead of above 4, when the GDP deflator terms of trade were used, as in the last chapter (Chapter 3, Equations 18, 19, p.115). d_u level required with 16 degrees of freedom at .01 level of significance is 1.09, so there is no evidence of serial correlation. We are not in a position to use these results for our forecasting analysis. Our objective is to compare our forecasts of non-food grain agricultural supply response with the actuals and so the period for the econometric estimates has to exclude the forecast period. It is only if this is done that the forecasts from the model will be comparable with the actuals.

The econometric model of the last chapter described above is re-estimated for the period 1980/81-1995/96. We begin with the acreage response curves estimated by us. We use both the log linear and linear variants, which are as follows;

(3) $A_{nt} = 165.118 + 3.21\ TOT_{ct-1}$

(53.21) (0.61)

$R^2=0.68$ d.f.=13

DW=1.93 Adj R^2 = 0.66

The d_u value for 13 degrees of freedom, at .005 level of significance is 1.34, so there is no evidence of serial correlation.

The log-lin estimates for this are as follows and confirm the results:

(4) $\text{Log } A_{nt} = 10.08+1.02\ TOT_{ct-1}$

(0.46) (0.01)

$R^2=.686$ d.f. =13

DW=1.92 Adj R^2 =0.67

The elasticity of acreage response is reasonable at 1.02, when the TOT variable is at 1.0. The d_u level of 1.92 shows no evidence of serial correlation.

In an alternate estimate we directly estimated the supply equation which is as follows:

(5) $Q_{nt}/A_{nt=}\ 42.21+251.78TOT_{ct}+0.55F/A_{nt}-32.68I/A_{nt}$

(27.29) (166.38) (4.26) (27.29)

$R^2=0.93$ d.f.=11

The additional variables are

Q=Gross output at constant prices; F=Fertiliser use in nitrogen equivalent tonnes; I=Gross irrigated area.

The regression is significant but none of the variables are, on account of multicollinearity. The simple test of multicollinearity proves this in this case since the correlation matrix of independent variables is as follows:

I/A_{nt} F/A_{nt}

$\underline{F/A_{nt}}$ 0.96

$\underline{TOT_{ct}}$ 0.72 0.82

With values of correlation coefficients above 0.9 between independent variables, no further testing is required for multicollinearity (Gujarati, 1995: 335-336).

One of the better methods of handling multicollinearity is improved specification of the equation systems (Gujarati, 1995: 340). As standard texts bring out dropping variables is not. For example, in the instant case dropping of either fertiliser or irrigation, strongly correlated with each other would be mis-specification. A recursive system, which we had specified in Chapter 3 and detailed below is a better specification, and therefore, takes care of the causality problem.

Supply (S_t) in any period would equal acreage in the period multiplied by yield in the period. Therefore,

$\log S_t = \log A_t + \log Y_t$

but

$A_t = a + b P_{t-1}$

where P is a relative price or terms of trade variable or

the logarithmic or log lin estimate for this will be

$\log A_t = \log a + b \log P_{t-1}$

or $\log A_t = a + bP_{t-1}$

and yield will be estimated as

$\log Y_t = a + bt$

This model will be a causal chain model of the type described earlier. (Ch.3). These kind of systems are also associated with causal chain analysis as pioneered by Wold (1953). The two crucial features of a recursive system are a triangular B matrix and a diagonal S matrix. As an illustration consider the model

$y_{1t} + d_{11}X_t = u_{1t}$

$b_{21}y_{1t} + y_{2t} + d_{21}X_t = u_{2t}$

with the specification

$$E(uu') = \Sigma = \begin{bmatrix} \sigma_{11} & 0 \\ 0 & \sigma_{22} \end{bmatrix}$$

To explore the connection between the y's and the u's we look at the reduced-form equations which are

$y_{1t}=-d_{11}x_t+u_t$

$y_{2t}=(b_{21}d_{11}-d_{21})x_t+(u_{2t}-b_{21}u_{1t})$

The first equation is the same in each case. Since the exogenous variable x is by assumption uncorrelated with the u's, the first equation may be estimated consistently by OLS. The second reduced-form equation shows y_{2t}, to be a function of both u_{1t} and u_{2t}. Thus, it would be inappropriate to estimate the second structural equation by an OLS regression of y, on y_2 and x. However, y_{1t} is uncorrelated with u_{2t}, since it is a function only of u_{1t} which has zero correlation with u_{2t}. Thus, an OLS regression of y_2 on y_1 and x will yield consistent estimates of the second structural equation.

It is obvious that if we ignore the errors specification, for in our case there is no reason for productivity to be correlated with acreage response, and treat this as an exactly specified model, acreage could be estimated from the first equation, plugged into the second equation and together with a trend yield equation, supply can be projected.

We use the variant where the period upto 1995/96 is used for building the estimates because the period 1996/97 to 2002/03 is the forecast period. Using the log lin model the acreage forecasts are as in Table 4.1. The TOT variable is as estimated by the CACP for the period 1996/97 to 2001/02. These estimates are as follows:

Table 4.1

Acreage Forecasts using the Log Lin Model

Year	*TOT for Agriculture*
1996/97	103.1
1997/98	105.6
1998/99	105.2
1999/2000	102.7
2000/01	102.8
2001/02	102.3

Source: CACP, 2003/04, Table 4.1, p.333. Figure for 2001/02 is provisional.

Given these estimates, we use the equations estimated (Equations 3 and 4 above) to estimate the acreage under non-food grain crops for the period 1996/97 to 2002/03.

The estimates derived from the log lin equation are designated as Acreagelo in Table 4.1 and those estimated from the linear equation are designated as Acreageli in the same table. Acreagelo and Acreageli can be compared with the actual acreage, which is designated as Acrgact.

Table 4.2

Acreage and Supply under Non-Food Grains Sector Forecasts and Actuals

Acreage, Supply and Yield are in Index Numbers (1981/82=100)

Year	*Acreagelo*	*Acreageli*	*Yieldlo*	*Supplylo*	*Supplyli*	*Supplyact*	*Acrgact*	*Yldact*
1997/98	136.3	125	133.75	182.3	167.19	181.6	133.6	132.3
1998/99	175.6	129.3	134.08	235.45	173.37	200.2	134.8	141.1
1999/2000	169.1	128.6	134.79	227.93	173.34	189	130.7	136.4
2000/01	132.4	124.4	135.57	179.5	168.65	178.2	127	133.2
2001/02	133.6	124.5	136.11	181.84	169.46	189.4	127.6	139.2
2002/03	127.1	123.7	136.73	173.78	169.15	168.4	115	127.3

Note: Acreaglo=Acreage under non-food grains estimated from log lin equation.

Acreageli=Acreage index under non-food grains estimated from linear equation.

Yieldlo=Yield index of non-food grains estimated from semi log yield trend.

Yieldli= Yield index for non-food grains estimated from linear area and yield forecasts.

Supplylo= Supply index for non-food grains estimated from log lin area and semi log yield forecasts.

Supplyli= Supply index for non-food grains estimated from linear area and yield forecasts.

Supplyact, Acrgact, Yldact are actual indices of supply, acreage and yield of non-food grains.

With the log lin cobweb, in the forecast period there are large swings in the forecast acreages which go up from 136.3 points in 1997/1998 to 175.6 points in 1998/99 in the acreage index and then go down to 127.1 points in 2002/03. (The Index Numbers are estimated with a base level of 1981/82=100.) Meanwhile the actual index of acreage fluctuates between 133.6 in 1997/98, 134.8 in 1998/99, going down to 115 in 2002/03. The log lin cobweb model (Equation 4 above) actually anticipates the direction of change in every year as shown in actual experience and to that extent is an interesting tool, in the sense it can forecast the nature of movement in acreage in the cycle i.e., whether there will be a contractionary or expansionary movement and this is an analytical plus point. It is easy in theory to show that a cobweb depicts oscillations. It is difficult to numerically demonstrate them. Thus, a model tracking a cycle is an achievement. But the magnitude of swings it estimates are more than the actual swings. Figure 4.1 below shows this graphically. The direction of movement in Acreagelo and Acreageact are the same. The fluctuations in Acreagelo curve are much higher than in the Acreageact curve.

Figure 4.1

Acreage Projections and Actuals

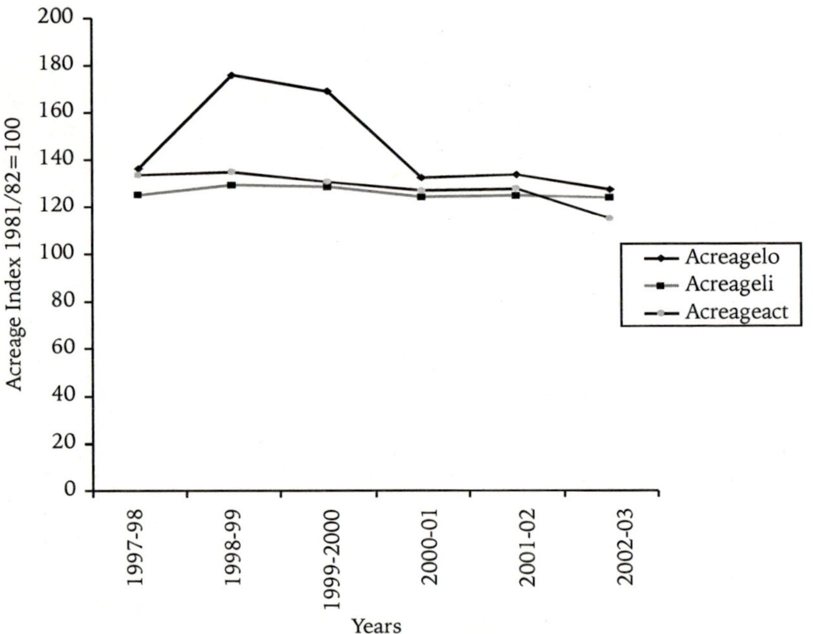

The linear model Acreageli estimates that the Index of Acreage goes down from 125 in 1997/98 to 129.3 in 1998/99 and then goes down to 123.7 in 2002/03. Again the linear model forecasts the direction of change correctly in every year and in that sense the cobweb estimated with linear equations, can be called a robust forecasting tool (Equation 3 above). It also shows much smaller swings than the log lin equation. In fact the quantitative swings it estimates are smaller than the actuals.

Figure 4.1 again shows that the Acreageli curve shows the same directional movements as the Acreageact curve.

Supply Projections

The yield of non-food grains is estimated from the index numbers of yield as follows:

$$\log Y_t = 97.43 + 1.023\, t$$

Where Y is the index of yield of non-food grains (1981/82=100)

And t = time 1981/82=1 (See Chapter 1 and 3).

The yield projections and actuals for the period 1997/98 to 2002/03 are contained in Table 4.1.

We estimate acreage from the lag equation and with the acreage and predicted yield figures from the trend line estimate the supply variable. Supply as estimated from the log lin and linear acreage response figures is estimated as a forecast variable in Table 4.1. Actual supply figures are also given for the relevant period, i.e., 1997/98 to 2002/03. There was a cycle in the actual supply curve for non-food grains in the period 1997/98 to 2002/03. The index went up from 181.6 in 1997/98 to 200.2 in 1998/99, went down to 169.4 in 2002/03. The supply curve using the log lin acreage response curve tracks this cycle in terms of downturns and recoveries but forecasts larger swings than the actual cycle. The supply index goes up from 182.3 in 1997/98 to 235.45 in 1998/99 and falls to 173.78 in 2002/03. Interestingly, the projected and actual figures are close in the period since 2000/01. These features stand out sharply in Figure 4.2 which shows Supplylo, which is the log lin variant.

The linear supply projection again catches the cyclical variations but the cycle is now largely damped and the terminal year is not below the originating year as in the actuals and as tracked by the log lin model. This feature also shows up in the Figure 4.3 showing the linear model Supply projection Supplyli. Figure 4.3 also shows Supplyli as almost a flat curve. To an extent the difficulty in forecasting exact quantities emerges from the fact that since 1995, Indian agriculture has been going through a below trend crisis period performance, which is difficult to track with time series tools.

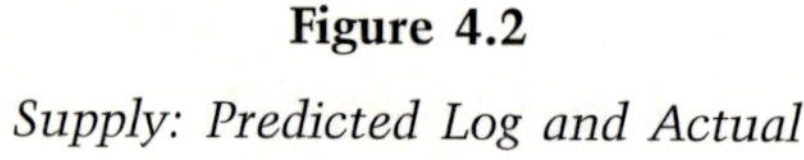

Figure 4.2

Supply: Predicted Log and Actual

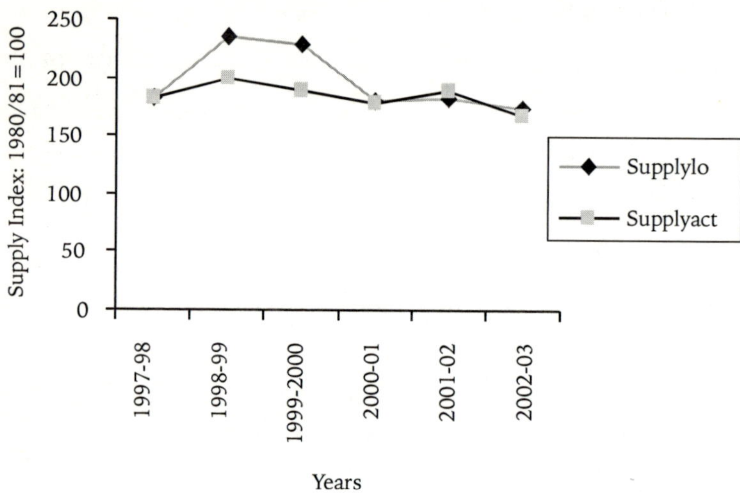

Conclusion

Forecasting is an essential test of the usefulness of an econometric exercise. A number of alternatives can be hypothesised to explain economic phenomenon but not all of them will stand the test of empirical verification. In the instant case the problem was more complicated on account of a transitional policy regime. The cobweb model worked as an explanation of significant parts of India's agrarian economy. For forecasting supply we found that a causal chain system which models the farmer's behaviour in terms of tracking his decision profile works. The farmer makes his acreage allocation decisions based on last year's prices and his technology is determined by underlying factors which we summarise in trend growth of yield. The sequential in a time sense use of the two relations gives us a reasonable method of tracking the agricultural cycle in India. We track cyclical movements accurately but not always their exact magnitudes. However, it can perhaps be legitimately argued that these applications of market-based tests to track the economy are an advance on our understanding of the Indian agricultural economy.

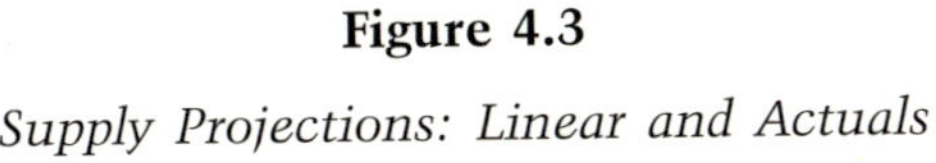

Figure 4.3

Supply Projections: Linear and Actuals

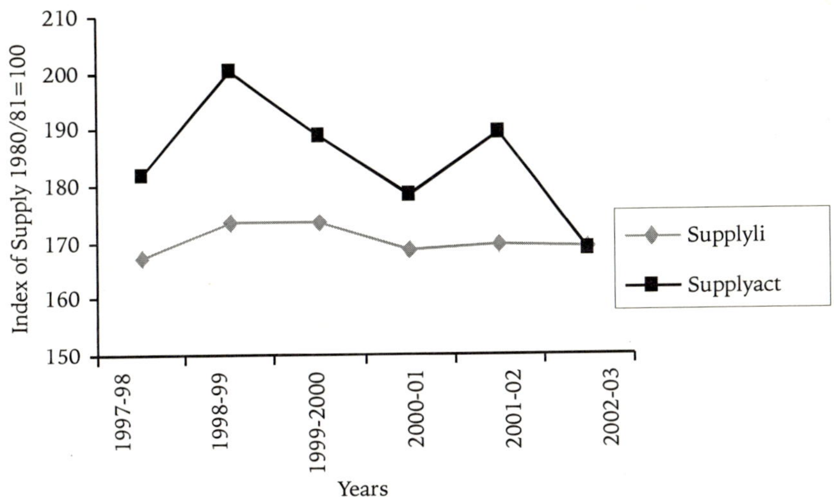

Effects of Intervention Policies and the Economics of Open Policies

The Theoretical Background

Classical welfare analysis refers to the use of supply and demand relationships to determine the level and distribution of gains and losses among consumers, producers, taxpayers and society from changes in economic policy. The technique is useful for policy analysts determining an economically efficient allocation of resources and determining whether it is appropriate or not to intervene in markets. (For details see Tweeten, 1989)

The technique is useful for analysts to estimate who gains and who loses from market failure and from the government distortions of markets. With appropriate modifications, classical welfare analysis is suited to analyse equity (distribution) issues as well as economic efficiency.

Concepts and Applications

Consumer surplus plus producer surplus equal net social benefit. Net social benefit is maximised at the equilibrium quantity under workable competition. It is important to note that the equilibrium price and quantity under classical welfare analysis depends on the initial distribution of resources.

There are many Pareto optima, depending on the initial distribution of resources before markets work. The global maximum net social gain which maximises the common good or utility of society is also a Pareto optimum.

The final distribution of net social benefits will be most equitable if the initial distribution of resources and access to opportunity are most equitable.

Given time, all resources become variable and values are bid up to remove pure profit. With producer surplus zero in the long run, it follows that consumers receive all net social benefits. This outcome is called consumer sovereignty in economics.

Classical welfare analysis is a powerful tool of economic policy analysis. It is sufficiently flexible to encompass not only social costs from an efficient output (foregone net social benefit or dead weight loss but also from an inefficient resource mix from excessive spoilage and administrative cost and also from lost output in resources "wasted" in political-economic seeking of transfers (PEST) activities.

Applications of classical welfare analysis include prices to producers p_p, to consumers p_c and at the border p_e along with an initial quantity q_e or q_1. It is apparent that Δq is approximately

$$=q_1-q_e \approx p_p-p_e/p_e(dq/dp^*p/q)_s q_1$$

where p_p-p_e/p_e is the proportional increase in price, and the term in parenthesis is the price elasticity of supply. The net social cost (value of goods and services or national income foregone) by the consumer subsidy is computed as $.5\Delta q\Delta p$. Values represented by areas can be approximated by recalling that the area of a triangle is one-half of the base (here Δq times the height here Δp.) where $\Delta p=p_p-p_e$.

Similarly, the net social gain by the producer surplus is computed as $.5\Delta q\Delta p$. Values represented by areas can be approximated by recalling that the area of a triangle is one-half of the base (here Δq times the height here Δp.) Where Δq is approximately =

$=q_1-q_e \approx p_e-p_c/p_e(dq/dp*p/q)_d q_1$

the term in parenthesis is the price elasticity of demand.

Other measures are rather easily calculated given the above estimates.

An Example: Cotton Policies in India

Cotton is one of India's largest crops, affected millions of farmers. It is a high cash input, risky game. The late eighties and early nineties sees the heyday of Indian cotton. Newer varieties meant lower crop cycles, less pesticides, lower costs and yields rose. India was exporting both the long and short staple varieties. The second half of the nineties saw a collapse. Output growth which was 2.8 per cent annual in the eighties, went up in the early nineties from 9.84 million bales in 1990/91 steadily to 14.23 million bales in 1996/97 but fell to 10.85 million bales in 1997/1998 and has been hovering between 9.5 and 11.5 million bales in the last few years. India imports a few thousand tonnes of raw cotton until the mid-nineties. This goes up to 0.54 lakh tonnes in 1997/98 (1 mn.=10 lakhs), 2.37 lakh tonnes in 1999/2000, 2.12 lakh tonnes in 2000/01 and 3.86 lakh tonnes in 2001/02. Some of the highest imports, around 20 per cent of domestic consumption, (1tonne =5.88 bales) have been in the last few years and domestic stocks of unsold cotton went up. A very nominal tariff was announced in recent years when the tariff rate for cotton was 5 per cent that too imposed in 2001, after large imports had taken place. It was raised to 10 per cent in October 2001. The situation improved in 2005/06 as global shortages emerged. The table below presents the ratio of imports to availability of cotton in India.

Production increased from 9.84 million bales (1 tonne = 5.88 bales) in 1990-91 to 14.23 million bales in 1996-97, registering an annual growth rate at 2.8 per cent. However, it declined to 10.85 million bales in 1997-98 and further to 8.72 million bales in 2002-03 before attaining a level of 13.47 million bales in 2003-04. India exported both long and short staple varieties of cotton during the late-eighties and early nineties. The country imported 0.80 lakh tonnes of raw cotton in 1994-1995 which increased to 2.37 lakh tonnes in 1999-2000. However, it declined to 2.12 lakh tonnes in 2000-01, increased to 3.87 lakh tonnes in 2001-02 before coming down to 2.33 lakh tonnes in 2002-03. Some of the highest imports, around 20 per cent of domestic consumption have taken place during the last few years and consequently domestic stocks of unsold cotton increased. As the international prices of cotton have fluctuated, so has been the behaviour of quantity of cotton imported.

Table 4.3

Ratio of Import to Availability of Cotton in India

('000 Tonnes, Percentage)

Year	*Production*	*Import*	*Export*	*Availability**	*% of Import to Availability*	*% of Import to Production*
1990-91	1672.80	0.00	497.14	1175.66	0.00	0.00
1991-92	1650.70	0.00	160.34	1490.36	0.00	0.00
1992-93	1938.00	138.13	63.74	2012.39	6.86	7.13
1993-94	1825.80	3.82	312.56	1517.06	0.25	0.21
1994-95	2021.30	80.80	70.75	2031.35	3.98	4.00
1995-96	2186.20	69.62	33.28	2222.54	3.13	3.18
1996-97	2419.10	2.92	269.58	2152.44	0.14	0.12
1997-98	1844.50	9.97	157.53	1696.94	0.59	0.54
1998-99	2089.30	57.40	41.96	2104.74	2.73	2.75
1999-2000	1960.10	237.40	15.91	2181.59	10.88	12.11
2000-01	1618.40	212.36	29.7	1801.06	11.79	13.12
2001-02	1700.00	387.04	8.23	2078.81	18.62	22.77
2002-03	1482.40	233.85	10.8	1705.45	13.71	15.78

Note: * Availability = Production + Import - Export.

Given the fact that subsidy on cotton exports in the world runs at US $320 billions, applied tariff rate at 5-10 per cent on cotton in recent years has been low. We examine the impact of cotton support at home and imports with low tariffs in the year 1999/2000 and 2000/01. The impact of policies is worked out on producers and consumers with the conceptual quantities spelt out above. The import policies and domestic support policies lead to a loss to producers of around Rs. 1500 crore if the farm level price inclusive of trade and transport costs is taken into account. Imports depress the realisation to the farmer at his doorstep. The effect of imports is a small gain to consumers as Table 4.4 brings out.

The argument of Table 4.4 is that in an era of large imports, particularly when the difference between domestic costs and prices and that in a foreign country from where imports are sourced is not large enough to be swamped by trade and transport margins, the impact of support prices can be counterbalanced by imports and the domestic producer can suffer losses from policies which simultaneously support domestic prices, but permit imports. Rows 3 and 4 model the effect of MSP on domestic prices both attempted and market prices which we have collected. But Row 5 looks at the empirically estimated farm gate price. Unfortunately, we could not get the particular years farm gate prices as they are not yet released by the Government. We made, we hope the 'reasonable assumption' that the relation between market and farm gate prices will be as in an earlier year when both sets of prices were available. If this assumption is not accepted, these calculations may be treated as a simulated experiment with available data.

Conclusions

Our main attempt has been to show that market analysis is important in substantial parts of the Indian agricultural economy. We believe that subject to the limitations of an individual researcher we have demonstrated this in abundant measure. We also show that simple econometric techniques can now be used to track oscillations in substantial parts of the Indian agricultural economy. Our cobwebs track the cycle in non-food grains acreages and aggregate supply. We catch the direction of changes on an annual plane. Some models also track quantities reasonably well.

Open economy macro economics in a partial welfare analytical frame can be used to model gains and losses of policies, which are now more complex than in a closed economy, in the framework of which we generally discuss policy in India.

Table 4.4

Producers Effects of Cotton Intervention Policies

S. No.	*Variable*	*Notation*	*Producers Units*	*1999/2000*	*2000/01*
1.	Domestic Production	q_s	Lakh tonnes	19.60	16.41
2.	Production Sold to Public Sector	q_p^	Lakh tonnes	0.86	1.03
3.	Government Producer Price(SMP)	p_g	Rs./qtl	1675[1]	1725[1]
4.	Effective Producer Price	p_p	Rs./qtl	1839[2]	1949[2]
5.	Farm Level Price	p_f	Rs/qtl	1440[3]	1484[3]
6.	Producers' Receipts (1x4)	$q_p p_p$	Rs. crores	360.44	319.8
7.	Producers Subsidy or Tax (4-5)	$p_{p-} p_f$	Rs./qtl	- 399	-465
8.	Policy Transfer to Producer (2x7)	q_p^ $(p_{p-} p_f)$	Rs. crores	-343	-479
9.	Proportional Tax (7/5x100)	$(p_{p-} p_{f)/} p_f$	%	27.71	31.33
10.	Direct Price Elasticity of Marketed Surplus			2.2	2.2
11.	Quantity Effect of Producers Tax (2x9x10)/100	q^$_{p-} q_p$	Lakh tonnes	0.0052[4]	
12.	Production Value Effect (7x11)/2		Rs. crores	-1037	
13.	Gain/Loss to Producers (8-12)		Rs. crores	-1516	

Notes: 1. Government of India, Ministry of Agriculture, CACP, 2002, p.237, average of J 34 and H4 SMP.

2. Government of India, Ministry of Agriculture, 2002, pp.161-162, average of J 34 and H4 prices.

3. The farm level price is estimated by the author. From the 1999/2000 price, the producers price for 1990/91 is estimated by using the wholesale price index of raw cotton price with 1980/81 as a base. This is estimated as Rs. 1199/qtl for 1990/91. This is the year for which published data is available for Farm harvest prices. See Ministry of Agriculture, Government of India, 1994. These are reported as Rs.774/qtl., Rs.1253/qtl., Rs.905/qtl and Rs.939/qtl, for A.P., Gujarat, Haryana and Karnataka, respectively, giving an average of Rs. 918/qtl. Thus, the difference between the producer or wholesale price and the farm harvest price is 23.86 per cent. This estimate is in the range of such differentials, as discussed by Kahlon and Tyagi, 1983. Applying it to the producers price figures in row 4 gives us the estimates of row 5.

4. Since the supply function is of a cobweb kind with an acreage response lag of one year, see Ch. 3, the impact of policy in 1999/2000 works out in year 2000/01.

Table 4.5

Effects of Cotton Intervention Policies Consumers

S. No.	Variable	Notation	Producers Units	1999/2000	2000/01
1.	Total Quantity Marketed and Consumed[5]	$q\hat{}_c$	Lakh tonnes	30.51	30.43
2.	Support Price	p_c	Rs./qtl	1675	1725
3.	Target Consumption Cost (1x2)	$q_c\hat{}p_c$	Rs. crores	5110.43	5249.18
4.	Effective Wholesale Price/Cost	p_w	Rs./qtl	1839	1949
5.	Effective Consumption Cost (1x4)	$q\hat{}_c\, p_w$	Rs. crores	5610.79	930.81
6.	Difference between International Price and Indian Price[6]	$p_{m\text{-}}p_w$	Rs/qtl	1.17	7.01
7.	Export Subsidy to Consumers (1x6)	$q\hat{}_c(p_m\text{-}p_w)$	Rs. crores	3.57	21.33
8.	Price Elasticity of Demand		%	0.60[7]	0.60[7]
9.	Consumption Support by Subsidy[8] (7x8)		lakh tonnes	0.23	4.21
10.	Consumption Value Gain[8] (6x9)x0.5		Rs. crores	0.019	1.48
11.	Consumer Gain[8] (7+10)		Rs. crores	3.589	22.81
12.	Gain to Global Traders[8] (6-tariff)		Rs. crores	3.41	20.30

Notes:

5. Total demand minus export as estimated by CACP: Ministry of Agriculture, Government of India, 2003, p.183.
6. Difference between the c.i.f Liverpool and Spot Mumbai price of Calif. Ariz and H-4 MP, comparable varieties. The 1999/2000 price is average of monthly figures for the period October-May and 2000/01 price is average of monthly figures for October to December. Figures as reported in CACP: Ministry of Agriculture, Government of India, 2002, Table 3.43, p.296.
7. The non-food grain price elasticities estimated in Annex, Table 2, give a weighted average price elasticity of around 0.6. This low elasticity number also looks plausible since raw cotton shares are to an extent technologically fixed in mixed fibre textiles, which are a large part of the total textile demand.
8. P. Krugman and M. Obstfeld, 2000, pp.198-199.

5 The Main Story

Main Findings and Conclusions

Background

The received orthodoxy in Indian agricultural economics with very serious and highly respectable parentage, is that while the farm economy is peasant based, on account of a highly distorted and imperfect market, prices have a limited role to play in it. This work attempts to re-examine this heritage. During the last quarter of the last century and more so since the eighties and nineties, significant changes took place. Newer institutions were instituted and policies were implemented. But the advent of market based policies was slow and the period was one of transition. Market based behaviour was, however significant in impact and expanding. This aspect needs study, structural analysis and examination of impacts.

Elasticity pessimism was the underlying accepted feature in the dominant approach in understanding the role of prices and markets in Indian agriculture. These *a priori* positions emerging from economy level views were taken while analysing the agricultural sector. C.H.H. Rao's (1975) classic work underlined that the technological base and distributive aspects of Indian agriculture determined economic outcomes. M.L. Dantwala placed agriculture in the rest of the economy in his understanding of economic development. Price policy, he says (1966) would depend upon the "view taken regarding the relationship and strategy of development". The need of necessity of a leading role of the state emerged axiomatically for the conditions of backwardness, inadequacy of normal market forces and the aftermath of foreign political domination (See for example, Acharya and Agarwal, 1994).

In that period, the aggregate agricultural supply function of the Indian economy was seen as price inelastic in the growth process. S.

Chakravarty (1974) treated agricultural supply as a constraint to the growth process and so did Dharam Narain (1965), G. Blynn (1966), A. Mitra (1977) and R. Thamarajakshi (1977). Dantwala while appreciative of the role of the market and prices in resource allocation and efficiency in agriculture, remained a sceptic on price response.

Alternative perspectives emerged. Kahlon and Tyagi (1983: 24) accepting the dominant position also questioned it. So, "the supply elasticities especially the short run elasticities, though positive, were found to be of low magnitude for most of the major crops in India. These findings have the obvious policy implication that price, as an instrument for achieving increased production, may have only a limited role to play" (Kahlon and Tyagi, 1983: 25). However, "there remain, however, complex questions as to the factors influencing the levels of farmer response to prices. The relative roles of fluctuations in area and yield, the effect on production of technology and weather, and more importantly, the fluctuations in response among regions of widely differing physical, economic and social characteristics, have become issues to be settled by further theoretical and empirical studies. Also for developing an effective price policy, the precise role of prices in stimulating total agricultural production and individual crop production as well as the overall effects of prices on savings, investment and production is to be known" (Kahlon and Tyagi, 1983: 25).

Meanwhile robust counterfactuals emerged. Beginning with Raj Krishna (1967), it was argued that at least at the crop level, price response was positive (Bapna, 1980). Elasticity pessimism was now questioned. Rajbans Kaur (1984) gave a 'balanced' picture. Mishra and Hazell (1994) and others now questioned the earlier tradition. Our approach, which was to examine the market responses of Indian agriculture in the reform period, built on the tradition of these later studies and scholars. The question we examined was the response to prices at the aggregate level in the Indian agricultural economy, for that question was of relevance in the policy reform debate.

Debates on aggregate trends of production and productivity in Indian agriculture are time honoured, for example in the works of Prof. Dantwala and Prof. Hanumantha Rao in the seventies and even earlier, but the good growth performance of the eighties is by now acknowledged

(Vyas, 1996). The demand aspect as determining the agricultural growth process is of recent origin. This led to more complex analysis, since different elasticities of demand, say of food grains and non-food grains, would underpin growth differently. Meanwhile, the so called crisis aspect of Indian agriculture continued to appear cyclically. (See the Ministry of Agriculture's (2004) *State of the Farmer*—volumes by Abhijit Sen, V.M. Rao, G.K. Chadha, G.S. Bhalla and B.B. Bhattacharya (Vols. XIV, X, II, XIX, XVIII) and the Mid Term Review of the Tenth Plan, Planning Commission, 2005). We can also outline this crisis by the work of Vyas (2003a).

Our study examined the record of production and productivity change in Indian agriculture to set the backdrop of the main analysis of price responses. This was then followed by the development of policy tools more synchronous with the larger policy changes taking place in India.

Objectives of Study

The motivation of the study was to find out the extent to which in terms of allocation of resources and output and productivity trends, the Indian agricultural economy showed the impact of price signals and response to market behaviour. The underlying assumption of the reform process was to postulate that the agricultural sector responds to market and price signals. Does empirical analysis verify the hypothesis that Indian agriculture responds at the aggregate level to price stimuli? Or does the agrarian economy reflect the transitional nature of the policy regime being followed, with some aspects responding to price signals and others determined by quantitative restrictions?

It is possible that allocation of resources to crops is price elastic only for the sectors where markets are allowed to function. This question arises since in food grains and external trade, there are still substantial government interventions, both of a quantitative and non-quantitative nature. It has long been accepted that at the crop level agriculture in India is price responsive. However, is it now true that there is a substantial sub-sector of the Indian agricultural economy which is price responsive? This kind of a hypothesis would be more substantive than the statement that at the crop level resource allocation was price sensitive, accepted for long. Do the underlying production, land allocation and productivity trends show that in the period of faster growth of the Indian economy and market reform, substantial agricultural sectors show the impact of income growth and of prices?

If the answer is positive to these questions, ignoring the marketisation of substantial sections of the economy would create both an understanding and a policy problem. We would then need to develop mongrel systems which are explanatory tools in the transitional regime. These tools (models) could then be used for policy analysis, both of a forecasting nature as also of a normative welfare gains type.

Does Indian agriculture show a changing nature and composition as seen from output and productivity trends across time? If it did, our questions would have a sharp edge. Our detailed analysis of the past broken up in periods would need to show that the growth and diversification of the agricultural economy and parts of it were demand determined (by the faster growth of the economy in recent decades) in large parts. However, in some crops technology and resource scarcities could still matter. Prices became important signallers for resource allocation, and this would need to be worked out in an empirical context.

Finally, newer policy questions would emerge from the analysis for the future. If prices are important it should be possible to explain the past with them, for the sectors in which they are important. To be non-trivial this would have to be for a significant part of the agricultural economy. If these models work, it should also be possible to use models with prices to develop forecasts for the future. Finally in the present stage of an open economy, agriculture economic analysis techniques could be used to work out the welfare consequences of trade policies.

Methods

For the specification of economic relationships, the analytical methods we used relied largely on economic theory as applied to agriculture and well known results like relatively inelastic income and supply parameters and lagged responses to prices on account of agricultural supply calendars. These were used to specify the parameters of supply functions and market response behaviour. For example, lags were used to solve the econometric problems of causality by specifying causal chain systems (Wold and Jureen, 1953; for more recent treatments, see Behrman, 1968; Klien, 1962; Nerlove, 1969; Waugh, 1969).

To estimate the structure of change taking place in Indian agriculture, in response to the pattern of economic growth, we use linear and semi-log trend analysis at the level of each crop. We cover a long period i.e., 1950 to 2004 and therefore periodise it according to economic growth epochs. We used the Chow Test to test if the periodisation postulated is in fact borne out by the data in terms of differential growth rates or different supply function parameters.

We develop two stylised policy experiments. The first is to use our work on the aggregate supply function to forecast supply of the non-food grains sub-sector of the Indian agricultural economy, to see if we can track the theoretical cycles of agricultural activity through empirical analysis. In the second example, we would use the structure of classical welfare analysis to model and obtain numerical gains and losses of government intervention policies in an open economy in a partial equilibrium framework (Krugman and Obstdfeld, 2000).

Main Results

The Big Story

Trends in output and productivity, showed that in the period of faster growth, from the mid-seventies onwards, non-food grains grew faster than grains as would be expected from demand theory. Chow tests confirmed this. Regarding food grains, there was a remarkable underlying stability in area and a rapid increase in yield. This was particularly so from the mid seventies in which we saw a much higher quantum of grains being produced with some land being actually released for other non-food grain crops. This took place on account of a rapid increase in yield. Indian agriculture came of age with diversification of the cropping base in relation, presumably, to demand arising from faster economic growth within the context of limited land reserves. This diversification led to higher growth in cash crops like cotton, oilseeds and fruits and vegetables. Growth was sourced by area and productivity expansion.

The significantly different supply features in the two periods, suggested differential responses to economic stimuli in the period of slower growth of the economy and the faster growth period. Also, they suggested that parts of the agrarian economy responded in different ways to market signals. Price incentives determined supply response in the non-food grains part of the economy. Econometric techniques could then be used for forecasting exercises to track oscillations in substantial parts of the Indian agricultural economy. Our cobwebs tracked the cycle in non-food grains acreages and aggregate supply. We caught the direction of changes on an annual plane. Some models also tracked quantities reasonably well.

Regarding the welfare aspects of trade policies, we examined the impact of cotton support at home and imports with low tariffs in the year 1999/2000 and 2000/01. Imports depressed the realisation to the farmer at his doorstep. The effect of imports was only a small gain to consumers as the figures on impact on consumers brought out.

Do prices act as resource allocators in the agricultural economy as it expanded and changed its structure in the growth process? Given the rich tradition of analysis in Indian agricultural economics, robust empirical analysis of price responses was required in a sector which is characterised by agro-climatic and calendar rigidities in the sense of lagged responses of outputs.

The dominant structure of economic policy in India since the mid-eighties was to first remove quantitative restrictions and replace them with fiscal and monetary policies, second to replace discretionary policies by rule based policies like low and uniform tax and tariff rates and attempts at reduction of fiscal deficits. It was obvious that in this context an estatist and strongly interventionist agricultural policy would be an oxymoron (Vyas, 2003). However, the reform process in the agricultural sector had to be knowledge based since the specificities of the sector are different and policy has to take these specificities into account. Sectoral responses and lags become relevant. This would require work to phase and harmonise policies in the sense of working out transitions to largely market-driven policies and ensuring consistencies between different instruments. This can only be attempted if analytical and empirical work preceded the efforts.

We showed that if the appropriate analytical and empirical work is undertaken, there will be an understanding of the emerging market profile of the Indian agricultural sector. Functioning economies are different from textbook models. Markets work in part and it is important to understand these specifics, in the sense of the part of the agricultural economy where markets work and the section where there are imperfections.

Trends

We found that trends in growth of area, production and yield were significantly different between the periods 1950/51 to 1975/76 and 1975/1976 to 2003/04, the last year for which data is available at the requisite level of disaggregation.

Regarding food grains, there was a remarkable underlying stability in area and a rapid increase in yield. This was particularly so from the mid seventies. Since the mid seventies, yield almost doubled. Area is constant in the period 1975-2003/04, declining in the *kharif* and rising in the *rabi*. *Rabi* shares of production have been rising. In this period, we see a much higher quantum of grains being produced with some land being actually released for other non-food grain crops. This takes place on account of a rapid increase in yield. Indian agriculture comes of age with diversification of the cropping base in relation presumably to demand arising from faster economic growth within the context of limited land reserves. Wheat is the crop of the late sixties and seventies, just as rice is of the second period. There has been, through the half century, a movement away from coarse cereals. This is largely taste and income determined since these are Giffen goods. By the beginning of this century, area under coarse cereals is less than in the early fifties. Output, however doubles in the half century. Area under pulses rises in the first phase and then stagnates. The output expansion in the second phase, significantly higher than the first phase, is sourced from yield.

Oilseeds are important crops of the Indian agricultural economy. They are in fact prominent in the rainfed and dry land areas and for a long period, irrigated area under oilseeds was marginal and is still low. Output growth rate almost doubles between the two periods. Yield growth expands four times from the first phase and in the second phase area and yield are almost equal sources of growth. Groundnut's output growth rate declines but rapeseed and mustard is the rising crop in the oilseed sector.

Until recently, cotton was a successful cash crop in India. Area and yield expansion was impressive. The second period is the phase of high growth in cotton. Sugarcane is a favourite crop if there is industrial demand for it, since it assures an income to the farmer. Production doubled in the half century.

The argument that in the recent period there has been a rapid expansion of vegetable and fruit crops is difficult to test on account of data difficulties in a long historical sweep. Potatoes are a crop for which reasonably robust data is available and its growth rate has been high all along.

The significantly different supply features in the two periods suggest differential responses to economic stimuli in the period of slower growth of the economy and the faster growth period. Also, they suggest that parts of the agrarian economy may respond in different ways to market signals, setting the stage for the analysis of aggregate supply.

Supply Response

Regarding agricultural supply, the emphasis was on models and empirical studies. We began with the theoretical literature on aggregate supply analysis, particularly the question on lags in response to price stimuli in the agricultural sector emerging from the time period characteristic of crop production. Given the seasonal nature of agricultural production, supply comes with a lag, depending on the crop calendar.

After much experimentation, we found from the Nerlovian acreage response function equations estimated by us that, for the period 1981/

1982 to 2003/04, the elasticity of acreage response to terms of trade of the CACP was reasonable at 1.02, instead of above 5 when the GDP deflator terms of trade were used. The lagged estimate for this period confirmed the results.

We postulated that the aggregate supply function for Indian agriculture would, in the light of the above analysis, consist of a price responsive non-food grains sector and a trend determined food grains sector with the farmer confident that government determined prices for grain would rise as in the past. The non-food grains supply function was recursively determined. This kind of relation is associated with Wold and Jureen's (1953) work (See a simplified description in Christ, 1966: 454-56). The first decision the farmer makes, in the light of market trends is to allocate land resources to non-food grains. After that, from the available technologies, he choses his input basket. Acreage is determined by the Nerlovian relation and productivity by technical change.

The acreage price elasticity was 1.02 and the trend growth in land productivity for non-food grains was 2.02 per cent annually. Thus, given the TOT values agricultural supply can be worked out for any year.

Policy Analysis

In policy analysis, we explained the traditional theory of economic policy in a simple fashion and then reviewed some of the policy literature, both at home and abroad. Finally, we give two applications of the tools developed in this work. We used the cobweb models developed to see if we could forecast aggregate non-food grain acreages and supply in India and use a partial equilibrium analytical framework to work out the impact of market instruments like tariff policies and domestic price interventions in the cotton crop.

In the nineties, newer formulations on policy structures in developing economies questioned the role of the state, once the agricultural economy gained in depth and size. D.S. Tyagi (1990) in a study on the managing of the food policy in India starts by saying that the most significant achievement of this policy was been a substantial increase in the economic and physical access to food. However, he also brings out limitations. More than a decade ago, D.S.Tyagi foresaw the crisis of 2006, namely that India has been importing wheat at prices higher than those offered by way of the minimum support price and in fact, subsidising imported wheat to sell it in the domestic market. This then leads to substantial welfare loss to Indian farmers. Tyagi said, "It needs to be noted that when the prices of wheat were high in the domestic market, even if the government would have allowed free trade in wheat and other cereals no net import would have taken place. This would have happened even in years when the world market prices were lower than the domestic market prices as the landed cost of foodgrains would have been much higher than the prevailing prices in the domestic market. Similarly when the world market prices were lower than the domestic market prices despite there being an excess supply in the country no net export of wheat or rice would have taken place. Thus the operations of private trade through the use of the world market would not have been in a position to bring about the desired supply-demand balance" (Tyagi, 1990: 175).

After examining recent studies by scholars like Vyas (2003a) and others, we also summarise the rich literature on policy studies abroad. Policy analysis for the agricultural sector is becoming a very powerful tool all over the world. In India, the tradition is just beginning. Tools of introducing uncertainty into the understanding of the agricultural economy and policy analysis are now very common. Uncertainty means the use of arbitrage, futures and hedging in price and stock-flow relationships. In the theoretical literature, there is a healthy mixture of well behaved neo-classical models with non-equilibrating models. (Anania and Mclalla, 1991; Antonovitz and Green, 1990; Lapan *et al.*, 1991 and Tronstad and Taylor, 1991).

The nineties also sees the introduction of open economy techniques in agricultural analysis. In the international literature apart from general equilibrium models, there emerge studies of trade and its impact as also of trade instruments, including tariff and tax policies. Indian literature also takes cognizance of open economy implications, although it was largely critical of trade impacts (Bhalla and Singh, 2002 and Bhattacharya, 2004).

We attempted to illustrate our analysis of some empirical relationships by stylised policy experiments. We used two experiments. The first was to use our work on the aggregate supply function to forecast supply of the non-food grains sub-sector of the Indian agricultural economy. The Commission on Agricultural Costs and Prices had already stated (CACP, 2000) that at the crop level these supply models would work. In the second example, we would use the structure of classical welfare analysis to model gains and losses of government intervention policies in an open economy in a partial equilibrium framework.

The logarithmic cobweb model, which we had estimated actually anticipated the direction of change every year as shown in actual experience and to that extent was an interesting tool, in the sense it forecasted the nature of movement in acreage in the cycle i.e., whether there will be a contractionary or expansionary movement and this was a very satisfying analytical plus-point. It is easy in theory to show that a cobweb depicts oscillations. It is difficult to numerically demonstrate them. Our model succeeded in tracking the cycles and this was an important result. The supply curve using the logarithmic acreage response curve tracked this cycle in terms of downturns and recoveries, but forecasts larger swings than the actual cycle.

The linear supply projection again caught cyclical variations, but the cycle was now largely damped and the terminal year was not below the originating year as in the actuals and as tracked by the logarithmic model.

In the second policy case setting, the theoretical framework in partial equilibrium welfare setting, we gave an example of cotton policies in a WTO trade dominated regime. Simultaneous pursuit of the impact of cotton support at home and imports with low tariffs in the year 1999/2000 and 2000/01 was a policy question of great interest, since such mutually inconsistent sets of policies are rare. The impact of policies was worked out on producers and consumers with the conceptual quantities spelt out above. Import policies and domestic support policies lead to a loss to producers of around Rs. 1500 crore if the farm level price inclusive of trade and transport costs was taken into account.

Imports depressed the realisation to the farmer at his doorstep. The effect of imports led only to a small gain to consumers.

The argument is that in an era of large imports, particularly when the difference between domestic costs and prices and that in a foreign country from where imports are sourced is not large enough to be swamped by trade and transport margins, the impact of support prices can be counterbalanced by imports and the domestic producer can suffer losses from policies which simultaneously support domestic prices, but permit imports. We modelled the effect of MSP on domestic prices both attempted and market prices which we collected. But we also looked at the empirically estimated farm gate price for this analysis of gains and losses.

Limitations of the Study and Scope for Further Work

At the analytical level, this work is only a beginning in studying the impact of economic reform on price behaviour and policies. The aggregate analysis completed needs to be followed up with seasonal analysis. The difficulties in terms of lack of availability of macro data at the agricultural season level will have to be addressed. For example, National Accounts categories will not be there. Further work with crop complexes at the agro-climatic level would be another direction of analysis. In some regions like Gujarat, coastal AP, garden areas of Karnataka and Kerala, commercialisation will be more intense and therefore, the price responses would be more.

Analytically another major avenue would be to model the impact of the open economy in agriculture. This has, as we saw in our literature review, been a major focus of international literature, but has been neglected in India. Open economy supply models, analysis of exchange rate, interest rate and tariff changes could then be studied. Finally, the welfare analysis we have done in a partial equilibrium frame can be extended to open economy general equilibrium analysis. Radhakrishna and Indrakant (1988) have studied price policy impacts in a general equilibrium model, but it is not an open economy variant and this could be attempted.

Bibliography

Data Sources Publications

Government of India (2005). *Agricultural Statistics at a Glance*. Delhi: Directorate of Economics and Statistics (Agricultural Statistics Division), Department of Agriculture and Cooperation, Ministry of Agriculture.

———. (2005). *National Accounts Statistics*. Delhi: Central Statistical Organisation, Ministry of Statistics and Program Implementation, Government of India, Conroller of Publications.

———. *Mid-Term Appraisal of 10th Five Year Plan (2002-07)*. Delhi: Planning Commission.

———. (2002). *Report of the Commission for Agricultural Costs and Prices for the Crops Sown During 2001-02 Season*. Delhi: CACP, Ministry of Agriculture, Manager of Publications.

———. (2003). *Report of the Commission for Agricultural Costs and Prices for the Crops Sown During 2002-03 Season*. Delhi: CACP, Ministry of Agriculture, Manager of Publications.

———. (2001). *Report of the Commission for Agricultural Costs and Prices for the Crops Sown During 2000-01 Season*. Delhi: CACP, Ministry of Agriculture, Government Press.

———. (2000). *Report of the Commission for Agricultural Costs and Prices for the Crops Sown During 1999-2000 Season*. Delhi: CACP, Ministry of Agriculture, Government Press.

———. (1994). *Farm Harvest Prices of Principal Crops in India: 1988/89-1990/91*. Delhi: Ministry of Agriculture, Controller of Publications.

———. (1984). *High Level Evaluation Committee*. Delhi: C.S.O., Manager of Publications.

References

Acharya S.S. and N.L. Agarwal (1994). *Agricultural Prices: Analysis and Policy*. New Delhi: Oxford & IBH Publishing Co. Pvt. Ltd.

Adelaja. A. (1991). "Price Changes, Supply Elasticities, Industry Organization and Dairy Productivity Distribution", *American Journal of Agricultural Economics* 26, February.

Ahmed, R. and B. Andrew (1989). *Rice Price Fluctuation and Approach to Price Stabilisation in Bangladesh*, Research Report No 72. Washington: International Food Policy Research Institute.

Alagh, M. (2004). "Aggregate Agricultural Supply Function in India", *Economic and Political Weekly* 23(2), January 10.

Alston, J., C. Carter, R. Green and D. Pick (1990) "Whither Armington Trade Models", *American Journal of Agricultural Economics* 72(2).

Anania, G. and A. Mclalla (1991). "Does Arbitraging Matter? Spatial Trade Models and Discriminatory Trade Policies", *American Journal of Agricultural Economics* 73(1).

Anderson, P. (1988). "Food Subsidies: Consumer Welfare and Producer Incentive", in J. Mellor and R. Ahmed (eds.), *Agricultural Price Policy for Developing Countries*. Baltimore and London: Johns Hopkins Press.

Anderson, K. and W. Martin (2005). *Agricultural Trade Reform and the Doha Development Agenda.* Basingstoke: Palgrave Macmillan and Washington D.C.: World Bank.

Anderson, K. and R. Tyers (1993). "Effects of Gradual Food Policy Reforms in 1990's", *European Review of Agricultural Economics* 19: 1-24.

Antonovitz, F. and R. Green (1990). "Alternative Estimates of Fed Beef Supply Response to Risk", *American Journal of Agricultural Economics* 72(2).

Askari H. and J.T. Cumming (1977). "Estimating Agricultural Supply Response with the Nerlove Model: A Survey", *International Economic Review* 18(2), June.

Bapna, S.L. (1980). *Aggregate Supply Response of Crops in a Developing Region*. New Delhi: Sultan Chand and Sons.

Begin, J. (1990). "A Game Theoretic Model of Endogenous Public Policies", *American Journal of Agricultural Economics* 72(1).

Behrman, J. (1968). *Supply Response in Underdeveloped Agriculture-A Case Study of Four Major Crops in Thailand 1937-63.* Amsterdam: North Holland.

Bhalla, G.S. (2004). *State of the Indian Farmer: A Millenium Study,* "Volume 19: Globalisation and Indian Agriculture". Delhi: Academic Foundation.

Bhalla, G.S. and Y. Alagh (1979). *Performance of Indian Agriculture-A District-wise Study.* New Delhi: Sterling Publishers.

Bhalla, G.S. and G. Singh (2002). *Indian Agriculture-Four Decades of Development.* New Delhi: Sage Publications.

Bhagwati, J. and S. Chakravarty (1969). "Contributions to Indian Economic Analysis: A Survey", *American Economic Review* 59(4), Part 2, September.

Bhardwaj, K. (1982). "Regional Differentiation in India", *Economic and Political Weekly* 17(14, 15, 16), Annual Number.

———. (1994). "Agricultural Price Policy for Growth: The Emerging Contradictions", in T. Byres (ed.), *The State, Development Planning and Liberalisation in India.* Delhi: Oxford University Press.

Bhattacharyya, B. (2004). *State of the Indian Farmer: A Millenium Study,* "Volume 18: Agricultural Exports". Delhi: Academic Foundation.

Blynn, G. (1966). *Agricultural Trends in India, 1891-1947*. Philadelphia University Press.

Chadha, G.K., S. Sen and H. Sharma (2004). *State of the Indian Farmer: A Millenium Study,* "Volume 2: Land Resources". Delhi: Academic Foundation.

Chakravarty, S. (1969). "Optimal Investment Policy in an Underdeveloped Economy", in H. Bos (ed.), *Towards Balanced International Growth*. Amsterdam: North Holland.

———. (1974). *Reflections on the Growth Process of the Indian Economy*. Hyderabad: Administrative Staff College of India.

Christ, C. (1966). *Econometric Models and Methods*. New York: John Wiley.

Cocherane, W. (1965). "The Nature of the Farm Price Problem", in H. Halcrow (ed.), *Contemporary Readings in Agricultural Economics*. Part 3, Chapter 10. New York: Prentice Hall.

Cramer, G., E. Wales and S. Shanganam (1993). "Impact of Liberalising Trade in the World Rice Market", *American Journal of Agricultural Economics* 75(1).

Dani, R. and A. Subramanian (2004). "From "Hindu Growth" to Productivity Surge: The Mystery of the Indian Growth Transition," IMF *Working Paper* WP/04/77. International Monetary Fund, Research Department.

Dantwala, M. (1962). "Price Policy for Agricultural Development-Rapporteurs Report and Summary of Group Discussion", *Indian Journal of Agricultural Economics* 17(4).

————. (1967). "Incentives and Disincentives in Indian Agriculture", *Indian Journal of Agricultural Economics* 22(2).

————. (1976). "Agricultural Policy in India since Independence", *Indian Journal of Agricultural Economics* 31(3).

De Cordoba, F. and D. Vanzetti (2005). *Coping with Trade Reform*. Geneva: UNCTAD.

Deshpande R.S., M. Bhende, P. Thippaiah and M. Vivekananda (2004). *State of the Indian Farmer: A Millenium Study,* "Volume 9: Crops and Cultivation". Delhi: Academic Foundation.

Dicken, Peter (1998). *Global Shift-Transforming the World Economy.* 3rd edition. New Delhi: Sage.

Duffy, P., M. Wohlgenant and J. Richardson (1990). "The Elasticity of Export Demand for US Cotton", *American Journal of Agricultural Economics* 72(2).

Evans, P. and J. Walsh (1994). *The EIU Guide to New GATT-Research Report*. London: The Economist Intelligence Unit.

Fulginiti, E. and R. Perrin (1990). "Argentine Agricultural Policy in a Multiple-Input, Multiple Output Framework", *American Journal of Agricultural Economics* 72(2).

Girliches, Z. (1959). "The Demand for Input in Agriculture and Derived Supply Elasticity", *Journal of Farm Economics* 41.

————. (1960). "The Estimates of Aggregate US Farm Supply Function", *Journal of Farm Economics* 42, May.

Goldberger, A. (1964). *Econometric Theory*. New York: John Wiley and Sons.

Gujarati, D. (1995). *Basic Econometrics.* Third Edition. New York: Mcgraw-Hill.

Hill, B. and D. Ray (1987). *Economics For Agriculture*. London: Macmillan.

Jodha, N. (1978). "Effectiveness of Farmers Adjustment to Risk", *Economic and Political Weekly* (13)25.

Johnson, G. (1949). *Forward Prices in Agriculture.* Chicago: The University of Chicago Press. Second Impression.

Johnston, J. (1984). *Econometric Methods*. Third Edition. New York: McGraw-Hill.

Kahlon A. and D. Tyagi (1983). *Agricultural Price Policy in India*. Delhi: Allied.

Kaur, Rajbans (1984). *Agricultural Pricing Policies in Developing Countries.* New Delhi: Kalyani Publishers.

Klien, L. (1962). *An Introduction to Econometrics.* New Jersey: Prentice Hall.

Krishna, R. (1962). "A Note on the Elasticity of the Marketable Surplus of A Subsistence Crop," *Indian Journal of Agricultural Economics*, July-September.

———. (1963). "Farm Supply Response in India-Pakistan: A Case Study of the Punjab Region", *The Economic Journal*, Volume 83.

———. (1967) "Agricultural Price Policy and Economic Development" in H. Southworth and B. Johnston (eds.), *Agricultural Price Policy and Economic Development.* Ithaca: Cornell University Press. pp.497-540.

Krugman, P. and M. Obstfeld (2000). *International Economics: Theory and Policy*. Addison Wesley.

Kumar, S. (1978). *Impact of Subsidised Rice on Food Consumption and Nutrition in Kerala.* Research Report No.5. Washington D.C.: International Food Policy Research Institute.

Lapan, H., G. Moschini and S. Hanson (1991). "Production, Hedging & Speculative Decisions with Options and Futures Markets", *American Journal of Agricultural Economics* 76(1).

Lapp, J. (1990). "Relative Agricultural Prices and Monetary Policy", *American Journal of Agricultural Economics* 27(3), August.

Leuthold, Raymond M., Joan C. Junkus and Jean E. Cordier (1989). *The Theory and Practice of Futures Markets*. Lexington, Massachusetts: D.C. Heath.

Mathur, P. and H. Ezekiel (1961). "Marketed Surplus of Food and Price Fluctuations in a Developing Economy", *Kyklos* 14.

Mishra, V. and P. Hazell (1996). "Terms of Trade, Rural Poverty, Technology and Investment: the Indian Experience, 1952-53 to 1990-91", *Economic and Political Weekly*, March 30.

Mitra, A. (1977). *Terms of Trade and Class Relations.* Bombay: Samiksha.

Morra, M. and G. Carlson (1990). "The Decision to Double Crop", *American Journal of Agricultural Economics* 72(2).

Morris, S. (1997). "Why Not Push for a Nine Percent Growth Rate?", *Economic and Political Weekly*, May 17-24, p.1153.

Mungekar, B. (1992). *The Political Economy of Terms of Trade*. Bombay: Himalaya Publishing House.

———. (1993). "Inter Sectoral Terms of Trade-Issues of Concept and Method", *Economic and Political Weekly:* A111-20. September 25.

Narain, D. (1965). *Impact of Price Movements on Areas under Selected Crops in India; 1900-1939*. Delhi: Oxford University Press.

Nerlove, M. (1958). *The Dynamics of Supply: Estimation of Farmers Response to Price*. Baltimore: Johns Hopkins Press.

———. (1956). "Estimates of the Elasticities of Supply of Selected Agricultural Commodities", *Journal of Farm Economics* 38: 492-509.

———. (1969). "Estimates of the Elasticities of Supply of Selected Agricultural Commodities" in K. Fox and G. Johnson (eds.), *Readings in the Economics of Agriculture.* Chicago: American Economic Association.

Panagariya, A. (2004). "Hindu vs. Reform Led Growth", *Financial Express Special*, Nov.7, p.2.

Pick, D. (1990). "Exchange Rate Risk and US Agricultural Trade Flows", *American Journal of Agricultural Economics* 27(3), August.

Pompelli, G. and D. Pick (1990). "Pass through of Exchange Rates and Tariffs in Brazil US Tobacco Trade", *American Journal of Agricultural Economics* 27(3), August.

Pyles, D. (1980). *Demand Theory and Elasticity Matrix Construction*. Chapter 4, pp.56-71.

Quiggin, J. (1991). "Supply Response Under Proportional 71's Taxation", *Journal of Agricultural Economics*, February.

Radhakrishna, R. and S. Indrakant (1988). *Evaluating Rice Market Intervention Policies*. Manila: Asian Development Bank.

Rao, C. (1975). "Agriculture: Policy and Performance" in B. Jalan (ed.) (2004). *Indian Economy Problems and Prospects*, Revised Edition. New Delhi: Penguin Books. pp.127-155.

Rao, V. (2004). *State of the Indian Farmer: A Millenium Study*, "Volume 10: Rainfed Agriculture". Delhi: Academic Foundation.

Ravi, C. (2001). *Complete Demand System, Welfare and Nutrition: An Analysis of Indian Consumption Data*. Ph.D. Dissertation. Hyderabad: Centre for Economic and Social Studies.

Robertson, J. and D. Orden (1990). "Monetary Impacts on Prices in the Short Run and Long Run", *American Journal of Agricultural Economics* 72(1).

Sawant, S. (1978). *Supply Behaviour in Agriculture*. Bombay: Himalaya.

Sawant, S. and C. Achutan (1995). "Agricultural Growth Across Crops and Regions: Emerging Trends and Patterns", *Economic and Political Weekly* 30(12).

Sen, A. and M. Bhatia (2004). *State of the Indian Farmer: A Millenium Study*, "Volume 14: Cost of Cultivation and Farm Income". Delhi: Academic Foundation.

Sen, P. (2005). "Modelling of Capital Flows and Foreign Exchange Reserves in India", *Economic and Political Weekly* 40(28).

Sengupta, J. and G. Tintner (1963). "On Some Economic Models of Development Planning", *Economia Internationale*, February.

Shepherd, G. (1968). *Agricultural Prices Analysis*. 5th Edition. Ames: Iowa Press.

Shetty, S. (1990). "Investment in Agriculture-Brief Review of Recent Trends", *Economic and Political Weekly* 25 (7 & 8), 17-24 February.

Swaminathan, M.S. (2006). "Foreword", in V. Vyas, *India's Agrarian Structure, Economic Policies and Sustainable Development: Variations on a Theme*. New Delhi: Academic Foundation.

Taylor, L. (1992). *The Rocky Road to Reform*. Helsinki: WIDER.

Thamarjakshi, R. (1977). "Role of Price Incentives in Stimulating Agricultural Production in a Developing Economy", in D. Ensminger (ed.), *Food Enough or Starvation for Millions*. New Delhi: Tata McGraw-Hill.

Tinbergen, J. (1956). *Economic Policy-Principles and Design*. Amsterdam: North Holland.

Tomek, W. and K. Robinson (1972). *Agricultural Product Prices*. London: Cornell University Press.

Tronstad, R. and C. Taylor (1991). "Dynamically Optimal After Tax Grain Storage, Cash Grain Sale & Hedging Strategies", *American Journal of Agricultural Economics* 73(1).

Tweeten, L. (1989). *Agricultural Policy Analysis Tools for Economic Development*. New York: Westview Press.

Tweeten, L., D. Pyles and S. Hennebery (1981). *Supply and Elasticity Estimation*. New York: West View.

Tyagi, D. (1990). *Managing India's Food Economy Problems and Alternatives*. New Delhi: Sage Publications.

Vyas, V. (2003). *India's Agrarian Structure, Economic Policies and Sustainable Development: Variations on a Theme*. New Delhi: Academic Foundation.

———. (2003a). "Economic Policies for Ensuring Food Security", in Mahendra Dev, K.P. Kannan and Nira Ramachandran (eds.), *Towards a Food Secure India Issues and Policies*. Delhi: Manohar.

Waugh, F. (1969). "Cobweb Models", in K. Fox and G. Johnson (eds.), *Readings in the Economics of Agriculture*. Chicago: American Economic Association.

Wilson, W. and H. Fung (1991). "Put Call Parity and Arbitrage Bounds for Options on Grain Futures", *Journal of Agricultural Economics*, February.

Wold, H. and L. Jureen (1953). *Demand Analysis-A Study in Econometrics*. New York: John Wiley and Sons.

Index

J

K

M

N

O

P

R

S

T

V

W